interesting books

Copyright © 2010 Fredrik Härén, Singapore.

Translated from Swedish by Fiona Miller

Publisher: Interesting Books — www.interesting.org

Official website: www.TheDevelopingWorld.com

ISBN 978-91-975470-7-9

To my **mother** and **father**

– and to all parents with a **curiosity** about the world who have bestowed this gift upon their children.

The **Developing** World

How an explosion of creativity from developing countries is changing the world

—and why the developed world has to start paying attention.

"If two people compete against each other and one is motivated and hungry but lacks the right tools while the other has both experience and tools, then it is likely that the one with the tools will win.

But what happens when the hungry and motivated person also has access to the same tools?"

Foreword

The idea for this book came about on a trip to India in 2003 – during an interview with a professor at the Indian Institute of Management in Bangalore, to be exact. I have, unfortunately, forgotten the professor's name, but I will never forget what he said to me. "Fredrik! We Indians don't want your boring jobs, like sewing footballs or assembling cell phones. We want your fun jobs: your research jobs, your analytical jobs, your design assignments and your development departments. Thanks to the Internet, we can look at what you're doing and compare it to what we're doing, and we've suddenly realized that there isn't such a great difference between you and us after all."

That interview was the turning point that helped me realize something was happening in the world. Later, at the end of 2005, when China's leader Hu Jintao announced to the nation that China was going to be 'an innovative country', I decided to dedicate a couple of years to really try to understand what it meant when developing countries decided to participate actively in the development of new ideas and innovations.

In December 2005, I moved to Beijing where I lived until April 2008, when I moved to Singapore. During the past few years, I have visited 18 developing countries in the course of working on this book.

My thesis is that **we in the Western world made a huge mistake when we divided up the countries of the world and defined them as developed and developing countries.** I do not mean that the label developed is in itself something negative:

A well-developed map can show the way.

An open parachute is ready to do its job.

A flower in full bloom can be admired in all its beauty.

Naturally, it is tempting to view the country you live in as developed – but I believe it is perilous to define a country as being stagnant in an ever-changing world. **By categorizing ourselves as being developed, we have given ourselves an imaginary straitjacket that stops us from creating new and better solutions; that hinders us from seizing our golden opportunities.**

By saying that we are developed, we are declaring that we are done developing.

By saying that we are done developing, we think that we have reached our goal.

When you reach your goal, you slow down.

When you slow down, you lose momentum and speed.

And stagnation is the same as the death of creativity.

I do not mean that the developed world has stopped getting ideas altogether, but we do not have as many as we used to. The ideas we do get are not nearly as innovative as they could be – and the changes that we implement are not as comprehensive, ground-breaking or original as they could be. We underestimate our creative potential by consciously limiting ourselves with the label developed. Believing that we can be developed in a world that is constantly changing is like treading water in a fast-flowing river. We mistake the moving of the legs for actual forward movement, when, in fact, we are just floating backwards. As soon as we stop swimming for a few minutes, we are whisked away by the force of the current.

It is tempting to think that we do not need to develop so much anymore. It is easy to think that we can take it easy. It is comfortable to believe that we are more or less ready with our work. It is understandable that we are blinded by our achievements. But it is a dangerous way to think.

A developing country is one that is always growing; one in which its inhabitants do not limit themselves by saying that they are done. A country that is still developing is alive and flexible. Something that is under development can be changed, replaced and influenced. A developing country is not confined by what 'should-be'. These countries are full of life. They have a feeling that they are creating something. There is a sense of direction.

Traditionally, the concept of developed and developing countries has meant something different. A developed country is, by implication, sophisticated, rich and advanced, while a developing one conjures up the picture of a primitive, poor and simple country.

I want to turn this picture upside down and show how dangerous it is to see your own country as developed; I want to highlight the advantages of living in a developing country - and to be a developing person.

I am fully aware of the fact that many developing countries face overwhelming problems when it comes to poverty, corruption, and lack of freedom as well as many other difficulties. I also realise that most leading research and development currently takes place in developed countries and that the Western world is light years ahead in many areas. And when I am writing about the development happening in developing countries I am not talking about the "underdeveloped" countries mostly in Africa, but of the developing countries that has developed rapidly the last 10-20 years.

Many people think that I am out of my mind when I say that, in spite of all the disadvantages that people in developing countries have, they also have advantages in comparison to those living in developed countries when it comes to creative thinking. According to these critics, I have overestimated the changes that are occurring, exaggerated the consequences and misunderstood where this is all headed.

I am not worried about being criticised if what I say in this book turns out to be wrong. It is quite possible that I am wrong and that the results of what is going on in the world turn out to be quite different to how I describe them. Predicting the future must be one of the most difficult things you can do. Or to quote Yogi Berra who said "It's tough to make predictions, especially about the future."

However, **the purpose of this book is not to describe an absolute truth, but to get you, the reader, more curious about what is happening in the world, to pique your interest about what these changes might mean and to make you more eager to implement the changes that you find necessary.**

In the course of researching this book, I have carried out more than 200 interviews; 100 of them were in-depth dialogues. I have spent endless hours on airplanes and at airports, and the passport I got at the beginning of 2006 was already full of travel permits less than two years later. The one I got in 2008 was full in April 2010.

I have met advertisers in Lithuania, professors in South Africa, marketing managers and entrepreneurs in China, an Indonesian minister, government workers in Singapore and industrial designers in India. I have had coffee with a young Art Director from Indonesia, who got her education in Singapore and then moved to Shanghai. I have interviewed a curator from Europe who recently started up a project to exhibit new Chinese art in Sweden. I have spoken with many entrepreneurs about everything from fish farming to MP3 players, and have had the honour of meeting fashion designers, journalists, PR managers, advertisers and many others.

I thought I knew what was going on in the world before I moved to China. But after spending the past four years travelling and speaking to people in different developing countries, I realized that I really had no idea of the scope or effects of the creative revolution that is going on in many developing countries right now.

I want to give another perspective on the world in this book and to turn a number of 'truths' upside down. Looking at the world from a different point of view lets you see things that you have never seen before.

Thanks to the progress in developing countries, the world is gradually getting access to many more creative people. This book tries to describe what these changes might lead to. It is my hope that you, the reader, will realize that something momentous is happening.

I hope that my writing can convey at least some small fraction of the wonder and fascination I myself experienced when working on this book.

FREDRIK HÄRÉN

I appreciate dialogue with my readers and would be very grateful for your opinions, thoughts, insights, questions and criticism on this book and the subjects it touches upon.

Please feel free to mail me at: **fredrik.haren@interesting.org**

Follow me on Twitter: **@fredrikharen**

If you read this sitting in a **developed country** I hope this book will **make you more curious** about what is happening in the world.

If you read this sitting in a **developing country** I hope this book will inspire you to look at your world with new eyes and to **trigger you to join the creative movement** that is sweeping through the world.

WHAT IS HAPPENING IN THE WORLD?

A look at the rapid development that is going on in the world at the moment and how the changes in education, technology, infrastructure and many other areas have drastically changed circumstances for us all – and especially for those living in developing countries.

When more and more people have access to **information**

If – back in 1990 – you had told people living in, say, Europe that within ten years they would have access to a technology that would make it possible to read 50 billion pages of information, listen to 10,000 radio stations, watch millions of TV clips, read thousands of newspapers, call and send mails to anywhere in the world, and have access to the world's biggest mail catalogue – and all for just 12 Euro per month – then very few people would have believed you.

Nowadays, most Europeans have Internet access and even complain that it is too slow. However, this does not mean that they have begun to use the Internet yet. Although they have access to the entire Internet, they use their bandwidth to read their local online newspapers or to visit eBay and YouTube and a handful of other sites. **Those who have really understood the whole point of the Internet are the people in developing countries.**

It is not until you meet these people and hear them talk about what the Internet means to them that you begin to realize what effect the Internet has on humanity. You might hear a young designer in Shanghai talking about his friend who learnt fluent Japanese by playing online Japanese games or perhaps a 28-year-old Chinese woman in Beijing describing how she learnt English fluently and then went on to study a free online program in feminism at an American university.

The 29-year-old Internet entrepreneur that I met in Bangalore a few years ago might also give you a hint about the significance of the Net. We ate a delicious dinner at a noisy Indian restaurant after I had completed my interview with him at his office. As we sat there in the outdoor area of the restaurant drinking beer on a Friday evening, I asked him what young Indians did on a Friday night. "I can't speak for anyone else," he replied. "But as far as I'm concerned, I usually read the online version of the Harvard Business Review."

The determination in his look made me feel slightly guilty about how badly I used Internet resources from other countries, sticking mainly to the sites of my own country or the USA as reference sources.

While the Internet means easier access to our own information for us in the developed world, for those living in developing countries it means access to information in general. People who hardly had access to any information ten years ago have suddenly got the same access to as much information as an academic in Boston or a journalist in London. Just as a hungry person appreciates food more than someone who is full, people who have had limited access to information recognize the value of the Internet more than those who have had a lot of information at their fingertips for a while.

Lim Tit Meng is a manager at the Singapore Science Centre and he told me a bit about how the inhabitants of developing countries have adopted the Internet. When he was at a conference in Boston a few years ago, Google had a stand where they showed in real time where in the world Google was being used most. It was two in the afternoon in Boston; in other words, the middle of the night in India and China.

"China and India were alive – like fireworks!" he explained. "They were these two big red blobs. And I thought to myself, 'Oh my god! It's 2.30 in the morning there.' The ability to access the Internet has really opened up everything."

The same thing is going on all over the world. A Brazilian whom I met at an Internet conference in Stockholm told me that Brazil has the world's highest usage of online social networks per capita, based on number of hours of Internet use per month. Although very few of the poor in Brazil have Internet access at home, the big cities have Internet cafés on every street corner where people can hang out. The sheer possibility of sitting anywhere in the world and being able to access the global mass of information means that, for the first time, people in developing countries can seriously begin to compete when it comes to creating world-leading innovations. The effects of this are going to be massive. As the Turkish-born Shanghai resident and designer Genco Berk put it so well in the jargon of computer games, **"The Internet is just one big turbo booster button."**

Hikmet Coskun Gunduz at the Department of Computer Science, Istanbul Bilgi University, exemplifies how the Internet has affected people in developing countries. At the moment, he is working on coming up with a quicker way of multiplying: faster integer multiplication.

"Before the Internet, I would have been forced to move to the USA because the world's leading professor in this subject works there," he told me. **"Ten years ago, I wouldn't even have had access to his work if I had remained here in Istanbul. Nowadays, though, I can chat with him every day if I feel like it."**

Hikmet Coskun Gunduz even has a mentor in Germany who is teaching him about European research methods, and who has also inspired him to translate Linux manuals into Turkish. In his spare time, Hikmet tries to solve one of the world's ten most difficult mathematical problems: P=NP or non-deterministic polynomial time. The Boston Clay Institute has promised to give a million dollars to the person who solves the problem and Hikmet is determined to be the winner. Thanks to the Internet, he can read how others have tried to solve the problem. However, money is not the main reason for wanting to solve the mystery; he wants to 'be a role model for other young Turkish people and show them that you can come from Turkey and still solve one of the world's greatest problems.'

A long time ago, when the old rubber barons in Brazil had the monopoly on rubber, they were indescribably rich. It is said that they even made streets out of rubber so that the noise of horses' hooves would not disturb the performances at the opera houses they built on their plantations. By controlling the supply of this sought-after raw material, they amassed untold wealth. However, a few rubber trees were smuggled out of Brazil and countries like Malaysia and Indonesia started producing rubber too. In the same way, we in the Western world have had a near monopoly on information and knowledge in many areas, but thanks to the Internet, this is changing.

You can really begin to grasp the impact of the Internet when one, for example, visits small villages in Sri Lanka and see children who teach each other how to use surf. You see, the Internet is not just a source of information and knowledge; it is also a tool. Someone just beginning to play World of Warcraft can get help from a more experienced player, and a ten-year-old boy can make an instructional video about how to use SCRATCH, MIT's programming tool for kids. An eleven-year-old in India can then use this film to teach himself how to program an interactive presentation for his school project, or to create his own version of Tetris.

This means that the eleven-year-old Indian boy does not need a programming expert to motivate him to develop his programming skills. Human role models no longer have to live in the same village. Ten years down the line, the Indian boy can himself be a leading programmer and part owner of a newly-started Indian software company.

We can already see the effects of this development. Cmune is just one example: a little software company founded by a Frenchman living in Beijing and an Australian in South Korea. In order to develop their software further, they then went out searching for extremely clever 3D developers. They eventually found a young man living in a small Tunisian village via an online community.

No matter that this was a remote village in a poor developing country: for one of the best designers of 3D models around was to be found there. He then became one of the top designers by learning from others on the Internet.

Most companies would not look to recruit employees living in small Tunisian villages. But it is precisely by such an example that we can see the changes that have already taken place. In ten years' time, we will not be talking about a handful of people in small villages as examples. For then tens of thousands of people will be growing up in a world where you can learn anything you put your mind to, no matter where you live, as long as your curiosity is alive and have access to the Internet.

However, perhaps one of the greatest benefits of having the Internet is not access to information and facts, but to sites like www.ted.com, where anyone, completely free of charge, can watch inspiring lectures by experts within a huge variety of subjects. From a professor in International Health like Hans Rosling, who passionately talks about how much healthier the world has become over the past few years, to brain researcher Jill Bolte Taylor, who gives a spell-binding talk about how the brain works.

A teacher I met on my travels said that the main task of a teacher is not to teach facts, but to encourage students to want to learn. **"Teachers don't get the horse to drink – they make the horse thirsty."** So, thanks to the Internet, young people – no matter what their geographical location – have both the tools with which to learn and the motivation to want to learn from the best and most inspirational people around the world. You could say that there are a lot of thirsty horses out there right now.

When many foals are inspired to become thirsty, then the right circumstances exist for the creation of countless new thoroughbred experts. And this process has already begun.

The battle of the **brains**

Professor Amarnath is the kind of teacher you wish all teachers were like: experienced yet young at heart, passionate about getting his students to challenge themselves and seize every opportunity that comes their way. His job is to help students at the Indian Institute of Technology in Mumbai become more creative – and he helps them do this in a creative way. According to Professor Amarnath, creativity is all about a sense of wonder, about being curious and astonished about everything you can do. He wants his students to recapture their child-like spirit, when they wanted to poke, investigate and build things.

During a long, interesting car journey between Mumbai and Pune he told me about the time he forbade his students to have their mobile phones with them on campus. When his students complained, he retorted by saying that of course they could use their phones - as long as they built them themselves. He has even started an innovation challenge in which students build football-playing robots. Although similar robot-building contests are to be found in many countries, Professor Amarnath realizes that even though Indian students have the same intellectual capabilities as students in the West, they may not have the same economic resources. So, instead of asking his students to build the usual five robots, which could then play football against five other robots, his contest requires them to build only one robot that can play against another one – but with nine footballs at the same time. This is just as challenging, but one that requires fewer physical and financial resources. **When the professor started the competition a few years ago, there were ten contestants, including himself. Nowadays, 15,000 students from all over India compete to create the most innovative football-playing robot, and the number of participants increases every year.**

The ACM International Collegiate Programming Contest, sponsored by IBM, is the world's most prestigious contest for university students. It is called The Battle of the Brains. In 2007, over 6,000 teams from more than 1,700 universities in 82 countries took part. As MIT (the Massachusetts Institute of Technology) in Boston is often given as an example of a 'super university', you might guess that they won this competition to find the university that has the world's best pro-gramming team. They came fourth – but they did not win. A good ranking even if they did not get a medal. The bronze medal went to St. Petersburg University of IT, Mechanics and Optics. Tsinghua University in China snapped up the silver, and Warsaw University in Poland took the gold.

In other words, students from developing countries won the world's most prestigious programming contest. Only three universities from developed countries made it into the top ten; the other seven came from developing nations. Apart from the medal winners, those that made it into the top ten include Novosibirsk State University, Saratov State University, Jiao Tong University and Moscow State Univer-sity. I could not help but laugh when I saw that Petrosavodsk State University just missed a top ten place and came in at an honourable thirteenth place. Petrosavodsk State University!? Petrosavodsk what?

I love it when my picture of the world is turned upside down and I find myself laughing out loud. If you had asked me fifteen years ago if I thought that Petrosavodsk State University would come thirteenth when 1,600 teams from the best universities in the world competed against each other in a programming contest, then I probably would not have said yes. In fact, it is far more probable that the top ten list would have looked completely different fifteen years ago with more teams from the USA and Western Europe at the top.

During this time, something has happened. I do not mean that Amer-icans and Europeans have necessarily become less intelligent – but rather that the world now has access to many more imaginative stu-dents as more creative people in developing countries have the chance to get an education in subjects they are good at. **The fast-growing group of well-educated people who can wrestle with creative prob-lems and who we can now connect with, thanks to the steep and fast increase in university students in developing countries, is such a powerful trend that it is difficult to get a good overview of what is going on.**

This same phenomenon can be seen in many countries and within many disciplines. After years of slow growth, creativity suddenly seems to have exploded. I have seen examples of this time and time again in many places in developing countries.

Take India's best design school, IID, which has been around for 50 years and always had one campus. Now, quite suddenly, it is planning to open three more in just a year. Five years ago, there were only five students in the industrial design course. The same course today has 20 students. In Mumbai fifteen years ago, there were only a handful of colleges where you could study for a Master of Business Administration, an MBA. At the end of 2007, you could find 42 colleges, and another 30 popped up in 2008. In other words, within a year, this Indian city had increased the number of its MBA programs from 42 to over 70. You can see the same kind of development going on in China, which educates five times as many engineers as the United States. There are 17 million university students in 2,000 universities. The number of Chinese in higher education is five times higher than it was five years ago and most of the students at these 2,000 universities are under the age of 20.

However, the rapid increase in college and university students is not only happening in India and China, but also in a number of smaller developing countries that have started to focus more on higher education. Singapore, for example, has decided to become a global hub for education in order to attract students from all over the world. Abu Dhabi wants to do the same thing and is building an academic city that will contain 40 universities and tens of thousands of students when it is finished.

In autumn 2007, when Business Week asked a panel of innovation consultants, academics and CEOs to rank the world's best 40 design programs, 25 of them were to be found in the USA. This is to be expected when it is an American magazine compiling the list. And, of course, the USA has been a world leader when it comes to design programs for many years. What is more interesting, though, is that only eight design courses from other developed nations (outside the USA) were mentioned, while seven design schools from developing countries made it onto the list of the world's best design programs. These seven were: ESDI BRASIL (Brazil), Hongik University College of Design (South Korea), Hong Kong Polytechnic University (Hong

Kong), National Cheng Kung University (Taiwan), National Institute of Design (Ahmedabad, India), Shih Chien University (Taiwan) and, last but not least, Tsinghua University (China).

New stars appear on the scene at a breath-taking pace. In China today, there are more than 800 universities that offer courses in design. It will be interesting to see who is on the list of the world's best design schools in fifteen years' time.

In a lecture that you can find on www.ted.com, Sir Ken Robinson talks about the increasing numbers of highly-educated people in the world. He mentions a UNESCO report that predicts that within the next thirty years more people will graduate than in the whole of the history of the world so far. A large majority of these graduates will be people from developing countries who want to get an education in order to compete on the global market.

Not all kinds of education boost creativity. In fact, the wrong kind of teaching is more likely to kill a student's creativity skills. One thing is clear, though, knowledge and information are essential when it comes to being creative. **I have put my favourite definition of an idea into this nutshell: Idea = P (K + I). In other words, an idea is when a Person (P) takes his or her Knowledge (K) and Information (I) and puts them together (+) in a new way.**

This definition shows that it is impossible to come up with a new idea from nothing. Knowledge about glass, how lenses distort light coupled with an understanding of how the eye works led to the invention of glasses. Knowledge about the zip and information about how the burrs of plants manage to fasten to your trousers led to the invention of Velcro.

All ideas arise when someone combines the knowledge and information she already has to come up with something new. If you study the formula, you realize the value of acquiring many different kinds of knowledge in order to have many diverse bricks to combine in different ways. And the more people who gain access to knowledge and information and who are then encouraged to learn how to put them together in novel ways, then the more creativity there will be.

You cannot, of course, equate knowledge with university. Many people acquire new knowledge and facts without going via traditional ways of learning and many spend years studying without really absorbing any knowledge. However, the rising numbers of university students paint a clear picture of the almost unbelievable increase of well-educated people in the world. As more and more of these people with access to knowledge and facts get the chance to combine them in new ways, then the more creative people there are who can come up with more innovative ideas.

According to Louise Julian, CEO for the educational company EF, a billion people are learning English – and 200 million of them are to be found in China alone. How can the world make the best use of this explosion of highly educated, multi-lingual and hungry academics? What will this mean in a wider perspective?

You need more than a seed if you want to grow a plant. The seed needs water, sun and fertile soil in order to grow. In much the same way, a country that wants to become innovative must have more than well-educated people with their heads full of information.

Innovation is about implementing change and ideas, and just because you have an idea that does not mean that you can make it a reality. Fertile soil is needed to help creative people implement their ideas. Until now, this has often been lacking in developing countries; but circumstances are gradually improving so that it is easier for them to turn their ideas into reality.

Show us **the way** to the moon

The people in developing countries have grandiose and daring dreams, but this does not mean that magical things with great impact will occur just like that. Inventive creation is as much about the ability to realize your ideas as about the ability to come up with them in the first place. What has been missing in many developing countries is the support that makes it easier for creative people to make their ideas come true.

When I interviewed Professor Raj Ramesar at his office in Cape Town University, he summed up the changes that are occurring rather poetically, "It is alright to gaze up at the stars and declare, 'I want to go there one day.' It is comforting to dream. But it is another thing altogether if you show me how to get there. What we need is someone who will show us the way to the moon; who will guide us to the stars."

Perhaps the most exciting thing that has happened in developing countries over the past few years is the fact that people, organizations and governments have begun to realize the value of creating this kind of guidance. Several governments have understood that they must actively help to support the creative branches in both words and actions. We should not underestimate the importance of hearing from the highest levels of government that innovation and creativity matter.

China's leaders realize that it is too expensive to import innovations from other countries, so that they are making an effort to develop their own instead. This concerted effort is known as 'Zi Zhu Chuang Xin' in Chinese, and can be freely translated as 'self-owned innovation'. When a president talks about the importance of creativity, you might think it is just empty words; but when Hu Jintao, China's president, encourages the country to become 'an innovation-oriented country within the next fifteen years', the people listen. In his speech, the president encouraged state-owned companies to support innovation more and the country as a whole to become more open to its own culture as well as learning from others. He added that 'profound social reform' would be needed in order to transform China into an innovative country.

We suddenly have innovation being officially sanctioned from on high. As a consultant whom I met in China put it, **"State-owned enterprises showed very little interest in creativity a few years ago. But all that has changed now."**

It is difficult for us Westerners to understand that countries like China can suddenly become creative just because the government has sanctioned it. Yet we can compare this to the sudden change that occurred when China went from being a totally non-capitalist system to being one of the world's foremost capitalist countries. It happened after Deng Xiaoping's famous speech in which he declared: "It doesn't matter if a cat is black or white – as long as it catches mice." In much the same way, China's leader has given a new speech in which he encourages the Chinese people to develop their creative skills.

A similar change is going on in other developing countries I have visited. In Malaysia for example the government has started to really support the creative industries. When I was one of the speakers at Design Week KL in May 2010 I saw examples of this. The KL Design week has only been around since 2009 but still they were able to get both a minister as well as the mayor of KL to come and speak at their different events. At the opening of the event the mayor of KL held a passionate speech where he invited the delegates of Design Week KL to tell him how the government could do even more to help. He said: "How can we support creativity? How can we turn this into a business success? How can we support those with good ideas to reach their customers?" And when I later met with some of the government representatives who are helping to spread innovation to Malaysian companies they too stressed how the government was taking an active role in developing innovation. With passion in her eyes one Malaysian government official said to me: "The government is leading the way. Work needs to be done. All governments have the responsibility to have a plan for the future." And she ended her short, passionate speech to me by saying: "We have to make it easy to make it happen.", and gave me a big, warm smile. The Malaysian government is really pushing to support the creative industries, and that is equally true for its neighbor Singapore.

At times, the multi-ethnic government in Singapore has by some been perceived as trying to squash creativity. However, a few years ago, it started being a country that actively - you could say, nearly aggressively – spreads the message about the significance of creativity. The government is not only investing in advertising campaigns and information packages, but it is also ploughing resources into government-run enterprises and departments so that they can construct an infrastructure that will boost creative development. Singapore has undergone a metamorphosis during the last three to five years. It has gone from being a relatively boring, sleepy and uncreative place to being a country that launches new initiatives in creative branches at an almost manic tempo. It can sometimes be difficult to keep up with all the schools, institutes, campaigns and ideas that are being launched. An old police station is being converted into a design school. New art and music schools as well as a centre for performing arts called The Esplanade have been built, and a gigantic new art college is opening its doors at one of the best addresses on Orchard Road. In addition to all of this, two enormous casinos have been built that will attract world-famous entertainment concepts.

Singapore has definitely decided to promote creativity through a massive, long-term investment in a variety of different areas. Similar determined efforts to create a more congenial atmosphere for the growth of creativity is taking place in many developing countries that have not traditionally been connected with innovation.

Thailand is more often associated with tourism and paddy fields than the boosting of innovation. There are, of course, always many sides to a country. When I was in Bangkok, I met two representatives from Thailand's National Innovations Agency, an organization that was founded three years ago in order to develop creativity and innovation. They told me that they had managed to breed a special type of clownfish that can be cultured in fish farms. One big advantage is that this provides competition that can help stop the illegal poaching of fish. Another benefit is that these tank-raised fish learn not to swim straight into the glass plates of the tanks. Another Thai innovation is synthetic diesel made from native nuts and a plastic substitute manufactured from local plants. Similar innovations can be seen in the most varied of businesses, from medical products to textiles. And yes, just three years ago, Thailand did not even have an organization to support the development of innovation.

The impact of this public kind of support is probably most apparent in South Korea. A few years ago, the government decided to work towards making South Korea a creative country that could export its ideas. One of its ventures is the DIC – Design Innovation Center – a kind of creative playhouse that contains everything from computers to 3D printers. People can come here with their ideas and develop them into innovations. These centers are often found on university campuses. There are 29 such centers in South Korea, five of which can be found in Seoul.

Hi-tech regions such as Silicon Valley in the USA, and technology parks like those in Heidelberg, Germany, and Grenoble, France, have now got competition from places like Dhahran Techno Valley in Saudi Arabia and Hsinchu Science Park in Taiwan—not to mention areas around major universities in Beijing and Shanghai in China, which already have the highest number of people in the world working in the research and development departments of global companies. Highly-educated Chinese and new graduates can easily get jobs there working in one of the research and development intensive companies that are located in these newly-built technology parks with all the latest hi-tech equipment.

One of these parks is The Knowledge and Innovation Community, KIC, located in the north of Shanghai, in the same area as top university Fudan. Nearby you can find 14 other universities with more than a total of 130,000 students. When it is completely finished, KIC will be an enormous technology park that attracts both small and large innovative new companies, started up by former students or researchers as well as housing the R&D departments of multinational organizations. Naturally, you can find all the mod cons that you would expect in a technology park. A fund of around 200 million US dollars has been created in a venture between Silicon Valley and KIC to invest in the start-ups that establish themselves in the KIC area.

Earlier generations of entrepreneurs from developing countries were forced to move to Silicon Valley in order to develop their ideas. Nowadays, the same technology, infrastructure and possibilities exist at home. Access to assets like cash and capital are also becoming more available, not least from those entrepreneurs from developing countries who have already earned a fortune in Silicon Valley and who now want to invest it locally. One such example is the Indian Sabeer Bhatia, the founder of Hotmail, who is now investing in IT companies in Bangalore.

You might think that the world's biggest digital arts festival takes place in London, Paris or New York – but you would be wrong. It is held in Shanghai. The Shanghai eArts Festival attracts delegates from around the world, from MIT in the States to the Pompidou Centre in Paris. They travel all the way to Shanghai. If world class digital art festivals are happening in China, how can one then say that Chinese do not have access to creative inspiration?

When I visited the eArts Festival in Shanghai I got to experience a lot of wonderful performing arts. For example, there was a troupe of dancers whose movements were recorded by a camera and then transformed into real time animations and shown on a gigantic screen behind them. I also saw a modern version of Beijing opera where the singers swayed in real time 3D on a screen, and a concert where the drummers and dancers were animated as fireworks on a screen.

I was amazed by the ability of the Chinese to combine thousand-year-old traditions with the latest technology. It was stunning, powerful and very impressive.

I also managed to take in a student performance: an installation where a bowl of water vibrated in time with the artist's heartbeat. In another installation, a tree trunk had been equipped with electronic sensors so that when you touched the inner rings you could hear a child crying; and when you touched the outer rings, an old man talked about his life. Although these installations could well have taken place in London or Stockholm, they did not. Students of electronic arts in

China's second major city have now got their very own world stage.

Considering how inspired I was by the little I managed to see, I wonder just how inspired the hundreds of Chinese students who took part were – and how this inspiration will affect innovation in the future. The fact that the best artists in the world in the field of digital arts get together in Shanghai punctures the argument that some put forth about the Chinese not becoming as creative as Westerners because of the lack of creative collaboration opportunities.

These days you can work with electronic art and sit in Shanghai or Berlin. You can be a designer living in Cape Town and not have to leave your city to attend one of the world's top design conferences. You can remain in Bangalore and set up your own IT company with the same conditions, or even better, than if you were living in Silicon Valley or near any European technology parks.

It is not only the physical infrastructure in the form of roads and airports that has developed quickly in progressive developing countries. Just as important are the massive investments in 'creative frameworks' during recent years. The soil for the ideas of creative people has become much more fertile in the space of just a few years.

I did not find the clearest example of how those in charge of developing countries have decided to develop their inhabitants' view of creativity in an art exhibition or a technology park, however; but in a cinema.

During one of my visits to India, I took the chance to see the film Taare Zameen Par in a new shopping complex on the outskirts of Delhi. The Bollywood star Aamir Khan, who even has a starring role, is the film's director. It is a film made in Bollywood that is not a 'Bollywood film'. It could have been made in England or the USA. Taare Zameen Par is about a small, Indian boy who goes through hell in school before a teacher realizes that he is dyslexic and a gifted painter.

At the end of the film, two women remained in their seats. I went up to them and started talking with them. It turned out that one of the women, Punita Tririkha, was herself dyslexic and – just like the boy in the film – had gone through hell at school. She had been beaten and bullied by teachers and pupils. Many years later, she realized that she was not an idiot, just dyslexic. A few years ago, she went on a course in jewellery design by chance and she suddenly found her calling in life. "I'm very successful now," she told me, before adding, "but I still can't read or write. I wish the government could force all Indian parents to see the film." In fact, the government realized the value of the film and subsidized the tickets so that more people could afford to see it.

There have always been innovative people in developing countries; but the fact that many of these countries have not stimulated creativity has created unnecessary mental barriers for many. The fact that India is putting resources into helping parents realize that having a child who can be an artist is worthwhile is just one example of how the government is trying to create a solid foundation to change attitudes towards creativity on a wider scale.

Another example is that a 'creative institute' is in the works to develop the creativity of all schoolchildren. There is also a national painting competition for kids where the President of India gives out the prizes. Together these small initiatives are slowly but surely changing the Indian people's opinion of the significance of creativity. When attitudes change, then new creative possibilities spring into being.

Could a film like Taare Zameen Par have been made ten years ago? According to Punita Tririkha, this would have been impossible. She went on to explain that India is undergoing a mental change process. I asked her what she thought India would be like in ten years' time if the change concerning how Indians view children, creativity and knowledge continued at the same pace for the next decade. **She smiled while saying, "When it comes to creativity, no country will be able to beat us. We are going to reign supreme!"**

If two people compete against each other and one is motivated and hungry but lacks the right tools while the other has both experience and tools, then it is likely that the one with the tools will win. But what happens when the hungry and motivated person also has access to the same tools?

When the framework for developing people's creativity is in place, it creates new conditions in which people can think. The construction of Science Centers, for example, shows how the opinion of developing nations about creativity is changing.

The world's **best Science** Centers

Science Centers are often seen as vital institutes for promoting children's interest in technology and science. They are often built playfully in order to inspire children to develop their creativity while also learning more about natural sciences and technology-related subjects. If you want to see what ambitions a country has when it comes to stimulating creativity among its young people, then you could do worse than look at the kind of Science Centers they have set up.

This was my starting point when I made an appointment to meet Assistant Professor Lim Tit Meng and Dr. Chew Tuan Chiong at the Singapore Science Center. Singapore has been criticized by outsiders claiming that talk of making the country a creative one is just empty words, and that developing countries cannot compete with developed ones when it comes to developing creative children's interest in technology and science. Dr. Chew Tuan Chiong disagrees. **"The center of gravity is changing and it won't be so easy for developed countries to keep their lead. We have changed gears and we will catch up before you know it."**

He is referring to the high ambitions of Singapore and other developing countries to compete on the global arena when it comes to developing the creative skills of their children. It has to do with changing the school system, investing more in culture, getting citizens to realize the importance of developing children's creativity and building innovative new science centers.

A few years ago, developing countries that built Science Centers made copies of the ones in the USA. "That is no longer the case," explains Dr. Chew. "These days every new Science Center thrives on being unique – no matter whether they are built in Dubai or China. Thanks to its size and wealth, the USA is still a leader within the branch in many ways. Their strength is the fact that they are still creative and know exactly which buttons to push to get the best results."According to Dr. Chew, the downside of American Science Centers is that they tend to take too much notice of what their American colleagues are doing, and so their science centers are too alike. In addition, they do not pick up on new ideas being created elsewhere in the world.

Dr. Chew also believes that Europe is stuck in the rut of its own history, which limits the development of new ideas. "Europe is too old school, even if they have a flash of brilliance now and then."

It is not certain that the country that builds the most innovative Science Centers will also succeed in creating the most creative children. However, the most ambitious centers in the world are being built in developing countries and they give the impression that these countries have stopped copying developed ones. They are now putting all their energy into coming up with their own solutions. The significance of this change is not an exaggeration and should not be underrated. "This shift in where the most exciting thoughts in the world are now coming from may be the most important change in the world too," continues Dr. Chew. **"We want to take part in and lead this intellectual thought development process. What's more – we are confident that we will do so."**

On my way out of the Singapore Science Center I saw hundreds of shouting, laughing children running between the different exhibits and being amazed about everything they discovered. The world is in constant change, but not everyone notices. When I asked the two men in charge of the Singapore Science Center what message they would like to send to the people in developed countries, their answer was quick and concise, "Wake up! Or you might wake up one day and notice that the world completely changed while you were sleeping."

An important condition for the flowering of creativity is the creation of institutes and other organizations. And, just as important, is the chance to meet other innovators in order to get inspiration and new ideas. This is why innovative individuals from developing countries moved to creative metropolises like New York and London. This is now changing so that it is possible to be similarly inspired in completely new places nowadays.

A part of **something greater**

Chris Lee was born in Singapore, and he is a born designer. He can design anything from a logo for a bank to an underground T-shirt, from a CD sleeve to an advertising campaign for a vodka brand. Chris refused a well-paid job as an Art Director in the capital of advertising, New York, in order to start up his own design studio in Singapore. His design company is called The Asylum and his company can be found in a old shop house in Singapore's Chinatown. He and his team work in the basement. On the ground floor, you can find Chris' shop where both local and international designers sell their products. In the evenings, he transforms the shop into a gallery, a lecture hall or a party room. You see, The Asylum is a design studio, a design boutique and design concept all in one.

So, why did he refuse the offer of a job in New York and decide to live in Singapore? "I'm sure I would have loved living in New York, but would my work have been more challenging and creative? I don't think so." Chris is well aware that Singapore does not have the same reputation as New York for being a creative hub, but he has decided to use Singapore as his base in spite of this – or, if you like, because of this. Due to the fact that so many complained a few years ago that Singapore was so dull, he felt compelled to change this point of view. Consequently, he has spent a lot of his time on developing the creative atmosphere in Singapore.

However, just because he has his base there, does not mean that he stays there all the time. At least once a month, he travels to another Asian metropolis to get inspiration: he might visit designer colleagues in Bangkok, clients in Hong Kong or a furniture fair in Manila. He feels especially inspired when he teaches design students. He is a guest lecturer on design courses in places like Mumbai, Beijing and the Philippines.

"Most students are very enthusiastic and excited about the future – everyone is trying to change things, make them better; and they are very curious and passionate. I meet this kind of positive energy everywhere in Asia on my travels."

Chris says that there is a big difference in how these young design students view the world compared to how he and his peers looked on the world ten or twenty years ago. Before, designers from developing nations had relatively little exposure to good design, whereas nowadays, they can choose from a smorgasbord of design. They also get the chance to meet excellent designers like Chris, when he is a guest lecturer.

Chris cannot remember exactly when he stopped saying that he lives in Singapore and, instead, started telling people that he lives in Asia with his base in Singapore. But he thinks it happened sometime during the past three to five years. This may seem like a fine distinction, but for Chris and many like him, it is an important one.

"When I go to Hong Kong and have sessions with designers, everyone is just charged with positive energy! Then I'll go to Shanghai where the same thing happens. There is a kind of positive momentum. At the same time, all the Asian countries are so different. The energy you pick up is different depending on whether you are in, say, India or Hong Kong. No matter where you are you get this sense of optimism and excitement. When you are in a place where everyone has energy, you feel energized yourself. And then you take that energy home with you and try to create something new and different. Maybe even start the next creative revolution."

No matter whether you are a fashion designer from Asia attending Fashion Week in Malaysia, an advertising executive taking part in a conference in Thailand or a film fan visiting the Pusan Film Festival in South Korea, this new feeling of being a member of the creative community in Asia has done wonders for Asia's creative self-confidence. Instead of being a clever yet isolated designer in Singapore, you are now a part of a community of good designers located in different places around Asia. Between trips, they keep in contact via the Internet, and as often as possible, they travel to meet each other in real life.

When low-price flights came to Asia little did people realize that airlines like AirAsia and Tiger Airways would act as catalysts for Asian creativity. However, thanks to them, creative people can 'hop' among the different creative cities in Asia, thus widening their horizons and contacts. Creative people in the USA and Europe have been able to visit different cities and countries for a long time now in order to get inspiration and new ideas. Now, thanks to budget airlines and the Internet, innovators in developing countries have the same possibilities.

"It's great!" Chris told me. "There is a feeling that we can change the world. I meet this attitude all the time and I'm really optimistic about the future. When these young designers learn to be savvier and feel they can design products that can be sold all over the world, then they will grow in self-confidence. All we need now are one or two people who can succeed in creating a global success, and who can then be role models for the rest of us. After that, our self-confidence is just going to explode."

If you know or hear about someone who becomes a great success, this can act as a catalyst and give you the feeling that you can succeed too. For example, when the two Singaporean photographers, Chuando and Frew Ow, won the assignment to style and photograph Janet Jackson for her record sleeve, photographers in Thailand and Indonesia did not say to themselves, "Oh – look at what great stars those photographers from Singapore are. If only we could be half as successful!" They thought this instead: "Oh – look at what great stars those photographers from Singapore are. If they can do it, so can we!"

While talking to innovative people in developing countries, it always strikes me how seldom they talk negatively of their competitors. A planner for conferences for graphic designers whom I met in Singapore told me how their Western speakers asked to be invited back year after year. The speakers got such a great surge of energy from talking to a group of like-minded people and being met by curiosity and interest instead of the suspicious scepticism that they often got at home.

The way they encourage each other to do better is similar to the way that cyclists group together during a race in order to work together to catch up with the leaders. Everyone in the group knows that they all win by helping each other. When the group catches up with the leaders, they become competitors once again to see who is going to win the race.

It seems to me as if creative people in developing countries have come to a subconscious decision to get together in a creative group and work together to catch up with the developed world. And I have met numerous creative people in different developing countries who are putting down their hearts and souls into project that will help to develop the creative communities where they live. They have come to understand that in order for their countries to compete on the global stage they need to come together. I have met a designer in Jakarta who saw his agency not as a company but as a school where he could teach his young countrymen how a world class creative agency should be run. I have met with people in Thailand, Indonesia, China, India and Malaysia who have started magazines targeted at the creative industries - not primarily to make money, but to help build a stronger creative community where good talent is show cased. It is people like the founder of Aesthetics Magazine in KL a magazine on art, design and creativity who wanted to show that great design can be made in Malaysia. He told me: "People come up to me and say 'I can't believe it [Aesthetics Magazine] is malaysian.' So I say "Why can't it be malaysian?" Vivian Toh, publisher, editor and founder of CUTOUT Magazine, another new design magazine from KL has the same ideas. She told me: "Me and a few other design professionals would like to rock the local design scene. It is about time we take the lead. The magazine's here to kick-start something greater, or attract potential sponsors to fund bigger design projects that involve the local talents. The local talents need more exposure and experience in order to think, create and design better things (design, products, campaigns, etc)."

The more creative people in developing countries see themselves in a context that is greater than just themselves or their own country, then the more they will be inspired by the ones who are already successful. And the more successful they are, then the more people they inspire. Just as many small streams coming together can create a fast-flowing river, so too can a number of scattered creators who suddenly begin to see themselves as a part of something bigger become a powerful force. This force will get stronger and stronger as the creative clusters in Asia increase. Naturally, this power will also decrease sooner or later

– just as it has here in the West – but it is important to realize all the same that millions of small streams are going to converge during the next few years. Many people in the developed world underestimate the effect that this creative flood will have as they do not fully realize just how many young creative people from developing countries are included in this flood.

The number of young creators is increasing sharply while, at the same time, they are beginning to define their world from a more expansive geographical perspective. What will the result be when these two phenomena meet? **What would happen if people from developing countries begin to identify themselves with all the other creative people in the developing world and then become inspired by these people who have already become successful?**

When the creative infrastructure in developing nations becomes better organized, the need for creative people to turn to the developed world for an outlet for their ideas diminishes. Instead, they will look to home.

Home sweet **home**

According to a professor I met in Seoul, ten years ago approximately 90% of Koreans who went to the USA to study stayed on. Nowadays, nearly 90% return home once they finish their studies. I have noticed similar trends in nearly all the developing countries I have visited. In China, people who have travelled to the West and then come back home, are known as sea turtles because just like turtles, they return to the place of their birth after a few years away.

30-year-old Sheila Tiwan is a good example of an Indonesian sea turtle. She moved to Silicon Valley when she was only seven. She came back to Indonesia two years ago and today she manages her family company Carsurin, one of Indonesia's largest independent inspection and consulting maritime companies and a Lloyd's agent in Indonesia. When I asked her why she – a young, ambitious woman in the middle of her career – did not stay put in Silicon Valley, she answered happily, "Because the opportunities are here in Jakarta." She went on to add that, although it may not be obvious that Jakarta can compete with Silicon Valley, if you stick around Indonesia for a while it is easier to discover the opportunities that exist there. According to her, young career people meet greater challenges; get more responsibility and more interesting work assignments faster if they use their skills in a developing country. In addition, she thought that the pace of life in the USA was too slow and that she was not allowed to try out her wings because she was too young. She felt as if she would always be spoon-fed there. After a few short months in Indonesia, she has already held presentations for venture capitalists with billion dollar portfolios.

"If I were in the USA, then my boss would have held the presentations. Over here I am trusted to do it myself. In a developing market, you are thrown into the deep end and have to learn to swim fast."

What Sheila means is that in a developing country you learn more in a shorter time, and quickly get the chance to develop the talents and skills you possess. In other words, it is easier to kick-start your career. Or as she put it: **"In a developing country, you develop faster."**

Sheila laughed when she told me about all her friends who had residence permits in developed countries, but who opted to come home after a few years. **"When you move from a chaotic but dynamic developing country to a developed one, your first, spontaneous reaction is, 'Wow! Everything is so nice and comfortable here.' After a while, most people get bored and go back home because everything is too structured; too perfect and complete."**

This is why Sheila moved back to Indonesia. Sure – she sometimes misses the American lifestyle where you can cycle to your local Starbucks for a coffee without getting dirty or sweaty, but when it comes to her career, she has much better opportunities to be creative in Indonesia than she had in Silicon Valley.

Silicon Valley has blossomed by attracting some of the best brains from around the world. What effect will it have on Silicon Valley if these people think it is more challenging and exciting back home in Jakarta or Beijing? And what will it mean for cities like Mumbai, Shanghai, Cape Town and Bangkok when young people find them as stimulating and attractive as Silicon Valley?

When developing nations have access to more creative people with good conditions in which to be innovative, then this leads to more locally developed ideas and innovations. At the same time, attitudes in developing nations are also changing when it comes to products from other countries.

Going from 'The West is best' to
'The Best is best'

A few years ago, a Starbucks store opened its doors inside Beijing's Forbidden City. It would be hard to find a clearer symbol of how a Western brand has conquered the world. For if the Chinese wanted to drink American coffee in paper cups while visiting the place that most strongly symbolizes their several-thousand-year-old civilization, then surely they would want to use other Western brands in order to prove that they are global and modern?

The phenomenon of Starbucks in the Forbidden City now has another meaning and the Starbucks sign can no longer be seen there. The wave of protests that washed over China about how wrong it was to allow an American fast-food chain to establish itself in the emperors' old residence forced the company to close down. Just because Starbucks took down the sign does not mean that the Chinese will stop drinking Starbucks coffee. However, it is a sign that people in developing countries have stopped equating 'better' with 'from a developed country' and have started looking at products on a more equal footing. Indeed, they are asking themselves more and more which product suits them best instead of just automatically buying something because it comes from the West.

National products are becoming more interesting too. For example, four years ago 40% of the songs in the top charts in the Philippines came from the West: from artists like Britney Spears, Westlife and The Corrs. Two years ago, only 15% came from the West. Top bands like the Black Eyed Peas and global phenomena like Robbie Williams, who will always be on the top of the pops, now find themselves competing for the top spots with local artists like Callalily, 6 Cyclemind, Sarah Geronimo and Spongecola.

Ahter Sonmez is a Turkish entrepreneur and music lover, who manages Turkey's largest DJ association. "I want to change the way Turks party," he said without a hint of irony. Turkey has changed radically in a few short years. Before 2004, many people in Turkey thought that a good DJ had to come from Europe or the USA. In fact, the phrase 'a good Turkish disc jockey' was a contradiction in terms. As many as 10,000 Turks could turn up at a gigantic disco and what decided whether the DJs were good or not were the countries they came from – not their ability to choose the right song or get people up and dancing. An exaggerated respect for all things Western contributed to this phenomenon. However, according to Ahter, things changed a few years ago and disco goers now have less respect and demand better quality.

Ahter himself used to make the mistake of believing that just because the world's best DJs came from Holland, then they always had to come from there. He has now begun to realize that completely different countries have just as interesting and exciting developments in this area - not least in his own country, Turkey. "Ten years ago there were, perhaps, about 100 professional musicians in Turkey," he told me. "These days the figure is nearer 10,000." These figures are probably made up by a proud and patriotic Turkish DJ, but his very statement is proof of a new self-confidence and belief in the abilities of his own country. He and his friends have begun to see that the most exciting development in the DJ business do not necessarily come from European DJs anymore as 'they have reached saturation point'. **As a DJ, he cannot help quoting Fatboy Slim and comparing the West with Fatboy Slim's greatest hits album Why try harder: "You seem to think that you are number one – so why try harder?"**

The day after my interview with Ahter Sonmez, I had lunch with Ekin Ergun, who is in charge of the Swedish Trade Council in Istanbul. She told me that a few years ago, you finished a night out in Istanbul by going to McDonald's because it was hip. Nowadays you are more likely to eat soup at four o'clock in the morning in true Turkish tradition. Naturally, people still go to McDonald's – but not because it is cool and American.

According to Ekin, Turkish brands are establishing themselves outside Turkey and new markets view them as hip foreign brands. However, most Turkish companies do not turn to Europe because of the old-fashioned view most Europeans have of what a Turkish brand is. Instead, these brands are focusing on growing markets that do not share these points of view – like Kazakhstan, for example.

I met the Indian designer couple, Aparna and Norden Wangdi, at their home in Delhi and they told me that all the hype surrounding everything from the West was beginning to abate. Just three to four years ago, buyers from the Middle East were only interested in clothes from Europe (or, to be more exact, European fashion brands, as many of these clothes are actually made in Asia). Since then, something has happened. **"These days 400 or 500 buyers from the Middle East come to India. They are still crazy about European fashion brands, but this is changing. It is as if they have suddenly discovered India and now they are going wild over Indian design too."** French and Italian fashion will still be sought after, but fashion centres like Paris and Milan now face competition from places that they would never have expected it from 10-15 years ago: places like Mumbai and New Delhi.

Hyoung-Bae Kim used to be a product designer for Samsung and now designs for his own company S-cluster. He explained how his customers' attitudes have changed over the years. Once upon a time, Korean companies would show him something Japanese and ask him to copy it. Then, a few years later, they said, "Make the product look Japanese or American." These days, however, they want products that symbolize the values of the company rather than looking like something else or as if they come from somewhere else. At the moment, Chinese companies are now ordering products from him that communicate what they stand for. In fact, they quite expressly tell him that they do not want the products to look American or Japanese, or even Chinese for that matter. They want their products to be creative and trendy – and reasonably priced. According to Hyoung-Bae Kim, only the Americans still want products to look American.

Increasing demands for products that are tailored to suit local tastes and culture mean more demands on manufacturers from developed countries to understand what customers in developing countries actually want. Requirements change when the largest markets for a product are no longer in developed countries but in developing ones. When people in developing nations no longer believe that products from the West are necessarily better and start choosing products according to other parameters, then the requirements change yet again.

The Western world has been able to survive due to the fact that products from the West have been regarded as better because of where they come from. As this 'truth' is being eroded, these products and services must now compete on their own merits. I wonder if we fully realize the implications of this. **If you take an advantage for granted over a long period of time, then it can be difficult to understand that you no longer have it.** Before, you got extra help when marketing brands in developing countries just because the brands were Western. You could say it is a bit like having a tailwind when you cycle. Nowadays, with consumers in developing countries appreciating local products, companies from these countries can be said to have less of a headwind. The sheer psychological effect of feeling that the headwind is lessening might just give the inhabitants of developing countries that little extra motivation and push them to try a little bit harder, which, in turn, will increase their competitiveness.

The number of creative people in developing countries is increasing while they are also getting easier access to the tools they need to foster their creativity. Outlets for their creativity are improving and it has become easier for them to implement their innovations on the market. In other words, more people are getting more ideas, while it is also getting easier to turn these ideas into innovations. The result? An explosion of creativity in countries not previously known for creating new ideas.

It's happening **now**

Thanks to the rapid development that has occurred and is still occurring, many developing nations are better equipped today than developed ones when it comes to inventing new ideas and innovations. A lot of people in the developed world still find this difficult to grasp. In fact, our picture of people from developing countries as being less educated, less creative and subject to bad conditions is something we have lived with for decades, so it is a deeply rooted 'truth'. And that is why so many believe that we cannot change this mental picture.

There are, of course, no absolute truths about people or cultures. People, countries, and cultures – they all change. These changes can be difficult to understand and they happen faster than most of us realize. Paradoxically, major changes can be difficult to spot. As Gordon Gao from the China-Europe International Business School said, **"It takes time for a change, especially a big one, to take shape. When you see a change and think 'Wow! Look at what's going on!' it is often already too late. The shape has already been formed."**

Transformations are especially treacherous when it comes to a paradigm shift. It makes it difficult to understand a change even though you think you have witnessed it. I call this the 'Kodak moment paralysis'. These days, an overwhelming majority of European and American adults have a digital camera or a mobile phone with a camera. One of the great advantages of having a digital camera (compared to a 35mm one) is that you can take as many photos as you like without wasting expensive film. In spite of this, very few adults take more than 100 photos at a wedding or a party, probably because we grew up with 35mm film. And although we know that we can shoot as many pictures as we want, we have not quite taken it in. We still go round waiting for those 'Kodak moments' as we do not want to waste film. In other words, it takes a little time before we really absorb a change and understand what it means. By being stuck in the rut of our old knowledge about taking photos, we have missed the most important point of digital photography: that is, that we can take endless snapshots.

In much the same way, people in developed countries run the risk of not understanding the effects of the changes going on in developing countries and how they are going to affect us.

Another danger is that changes creep up on us quickly. What I mean is that there is a risk that we choose to ignore a change because, at the beginning, the effects of the change are not as powerful as we thought they would be. For example, when the Internet made its breakthrough, many people warned that newspapers would suffer badly from dwindling readership. When this did not happen, many experts assumed that the danger had been exaggerated and that the change would not be as big as predicted.

Paper-based newspapers survived back then; but things have suddenly started happening. According to a report by Deutsche Bank, the value of American newspapers subscribers (calculated as income) has decreased by nearly 50% in just four years. Until a couple of years ago, there were eleven different IT magazines (paper ones) in France. In less than half a year, the figure dropped to just one.

The West has a tendency to underestimate the consequences of the growing creativity in developing lands. We might come to regret this – sorely. It will, of course, take countries like China and India a very long time to catch up with developed nations in terms of BNP per capita or whatever measurement you want to use. It would be foolish, though, to stare blindly at percentage differences among countries. By doing so, you are very likely to miss the actual changes that are going on. There are millions of people who are poor, lack an education and who fight on a daily basis for survival. Their struggle to create a better world is slow, thankless and often fruitless. A couple of hundred million poor people in the rural regions of China are not just a human tragedy; it affects China's per capita BNP or patent licences per inhabitant negatively. It also hides the fact that, thanks to the increasing number of university graduates in India and China, the world now has access to millions of well-educated people who can develop new ideas, thoughts, inventions and innovations.

The change going on at the moment is not complete. We are right in the middle of it and notice its effects even if they are not so obvious yet. Just as a pan of water on a stove shows very few signs that the water is about to boil before it starts doing so, so too do major shifts in the world occur without us seeing them. Understanding the changes is the equivalent of seeing the tiny bubbles that appear just before it is obvious that the water is boiling. At first sight, these bubbles may appear insignificant, but they are a sign of the much bigger changes to come. The traces of increased innovations that we can see in developing countries at the moment are exactly this type of small and seemingly unimportant changes. However, we should take these signs seriously. It is clear that changes are happening; you can see examples of this everywhere. The world is boiling with them.

Let us take a look at some examples of the changes happening in many countries around the world. In November 2007, the China Daily reported that China's investment in innovation would soon reap results when it comes to the number of people working to develop and protect intellectual property rights. During the next two or three years, China is planning to hire 2,100 people to work with the issuing of patents, 1,500 to work with trademarks and a further 4,000 to ensure that people follow China's IP (intellectual property) laws better.

Zheng Shengli, Dean of the IP Law School at Beijing University, reckons that there are about 1.5 million researchers at enterprises and universities around China. Of the 1,700 lawyers who work with IP law, 1,000 became qualified in the subject after 2001. These new resources will be needed as applications for patents have increased by 800% in China from 1995 to 2005.

Wu Yiming is a project manager at the International Creative Industry Exhibition in Shanghai, an exhibition for companies working in creative industries like design, advertising, communications and IT. In the course of his work, he has identified 75 Creative Industry Parks in Shanghai alone. His company decided to launch a conference on the theme of creative industries because they noticed a strong increase in interest among the owners of factories in the Shanghai area.

Wu Yiming told me that the factory owners had become rich by making products for companies in the West. Or as he put it, **"They've**

earned their first pot of gold. Now they want to earn their second pot, but this time they want to satisfy their egos." Their main motivation this time round is not to earn money, but to develop. They want to have their own products, their own trademarks and launch their own enterprises that go on to become known for their strength and uniqueness. They no longer want to be just suppliers: they want something to call their own. This is why they need product developers, designers, marketing executives and other creative people who can help them make their visions become realities. They have the money and now they want to invest it. Suddenly, a new market has been created: a market for creative services in China. This market has appeared about the same time as universities in countries like China and India seriously started to graduate students in subjects like design and marketing.

Where before suppliers in developing countries only produced items according to drawings they were sent from buyers in the West, these days they have begun to employ their own designers as well as tendering to design other people's products. This is happening in many lines of business, from Chinese manufacturers of store interiors, who are already taking over the design of store interiors to Indian software developers, who are no longer just taking care of support and repairs but who are bidding to develop new products too. One example of this change is the Swedish business application company IFS (Industrial and Financial Systems), which opened a branch in Sri Lanka to take responsibility for service and repairs. The Sri Lankan office ended up developing a whole range of the company's new products and services.

In a 2008 issue of The Strait Times, you can read about a local clothing company in Singapore that not only makes clothes for companies like Gap and Ralph Lauren, but that also flies its own in-house designers over to the USA to give fashion and design advice for upcoming collections.

Jez Tan is a designer for the Ghim Li Group and designs outfits for Banana Republic, Benetton and Macy's and Ivonn Law from SL Global designs for Gap, Esprit and Ralph Lauren. They are both under

30. Six years ago, the Ghim Li Group established its own design team while SL Group started up its team three years ago. They now fly their designers to New York, Milan, Paris and San Francisco to present their latest ideas. In other words, you can find not only sales executives from factories who want to make the clothes, but also designers who want to sell their own creative ideas.

Vytautas Ramonaitis from Lithuania is a telecoms expert. He gave me a good example of how the telecommunications business has been affected by the increase of creative telecoms companies from developing countries. "There is a company in Russia called NetCracker that produces OSS (Operation Support Systems), which is the heart of a telecom company's IT system. I first met this company when we bid for a mobile operating company in Lithuania. At first, they didn't seem to be able to offer anything special. They didn't have any services that the major American giants with thousands of employees and years of experience didn't already offer. The only thing they did have was the ability to listen to what the customers really wanted." Vytautas told me that he wrote a report to his American office to warn them about this new competitor, but in reply, he received a scathing e-mail message stating: "Those Russians are no threat. Just look at their US office – they only have three people working there." Three years later, NetCracker was the second largest OSS service provider in the world while the American giant that Vytautas worked for had to fire a couple of thousand employees, and stop their OSS production. They were even forced to merge with another company in order to survive. According to Vytautas, both companies are equals nowadays.

So, the old truth that the workforce in developing countries is cheaper but less creative is no longer true – as more and more multinationals have learnt, some of them the hard way. If multinational corporations based in developed countries want to compete with the new competitors in developing nations, then they will have to establish their own research units there.

Ten years ago, IBM had no product development at all in China; today they have 10,000 employees there. 30% of them work with product development, and of these, 75% have a Master's degree or a

Ph.D. Once I found myself in a lift with the HR Manager at Motorola in China, so I grabbed the chance to ask her a few questions. She told me that the company had 10,000 employees in China.

"How many work with research and development?" I asked.

"4,000," came the reply.

That means that 40% of Motorola's staff works with research and development. Major corporations like IBM, Nokia and Motorola would never have large R&D departments in a country if they did not believe they would reap creative benefits from their investments.

Another example of how creativity and innovation has exploded in developing countries during recent years is AstraZeneca: they get the most suggestions about how to improve things per employee from their staff in China.

In a worldwide advertising competition held in Cannes in 2007, there were nearly as many entries from advertising agencies in developing countries as there were from those in developed ones. So, when the world's best advertising campaigns compete, a large number of awards go to creative campaigns made for customers in developing countries by creative people working there. This is yet another clear example of how the creative standard in developing countries has begun to compete globally in just a few short years.

In a report, the research and advisory firm Gartner states the following: "Innovation from new, relatively untapped markets is driving global innovation, creating a force that cannot be ignored by organizations in mature markets. Organizations operating in highly constrained environments in emerging nations such as China and India are innovating at a faster rate than ever before." Gartner predicts that by 2015, developing countries will be responsible for 20% of what they call 'disruptive IT innovation' – i.e. an innovation that creates new and unexpected markets via a different set of values; an innovation that is so big that it eventually replaces the established approach.

It is also estimated that by 2012, 20% of all international patent applications will come from developing countries.

All in all, there are now many signs that developing nations can compete not only when it comes to price but creativity, too. So, why do so many people in developed countries claim that it does not matter if factories move to countries like China because they cannot compete when it comes to creative work?

Design guru John Heskett, a professor at The Hong Kong Polytechnic University, has worked with design in both Europe and the USA for many decades. He says that this is a way of ignoring what is going on. **"The developed world comforts itself with fantasies about keeping the upper hand within the creative industries while many other jobs move. America still thinks that it is the centre of creativity, but this centre is shifting. The West just hasn't realized it yet."**

Heskett issues a warning about what can happen if the Chinese succeed in combining their knowledge of low-price production with high-quality creativity. "If the Chinese learn to develop their cost-consciousness and can compete with quality products at a lower price, then they will have an amazing edge."

Amena from the innovation company What If in Shanghai has this to say, "It's happening and we're in the midst of it! You might have to look among the grassroots to see it, but change is there. Everywhere!" Pete Heskett from the advertising bureau BBH in Shanghai confirms this. "There is a creative revolution going on at a grassroots level at the moment. In any given week and in more and more cities in China, the number of fashion designers, graphic designers and other creators who are forging new markets for their products is increasing. We will soon start seeing the results of this on a global scale. Increasingly, we are going to be exposed to Chinese creativity. In fact, this is already happening although most people haven't realized it yet." This creative grassroots revolution can be seen in the most unexpected of places. A while back, I flew to Wuhan, a city with eight million inhabitants that I had never heard of three years ago. Wuhan is strategically placed on the banks of the Yellow River between Shanghai, China's financial centre, and Chongqing, a city with more than 30 million inhabitants. I was in Wuhan to give a talk about creativity on a management course for the top executives of China Mobile in Hubei Province.

China has over 100 cities with more than one million inhabitants, and people are working feverishly in all these cities to upgrade their technology and catch up with the 21st century. China Mobile, one of the country's largest employer, plays an important part in this. The company has focused on developing the skills of its managers so that they participate in the most up-to-date courses.

When the local HR Manager introduced me, she urged the audience to listen carefully as she said that this last session about business creativity was the most important part of their three-day course. After my talk, I was invited to have dinner with the senior manager of China Mobile in Wuhan, who had already heard one of my earlier lectures. He had asked me back because he wanted me to share my thoughts with the rest of his managers. He told me that I had inspired him to spread the message that it was important to dare to do things differently, and he confessed that he had already begun to do so. For example, the party they had held the night before was a little different to previous ones.

I wanted to know if the boss really had organized the party differently so I asked the person next to me if it was a different yet enjoyable occasion. "It was brilliant!" he said —except that he spoke Chinese and said, "Hen hao!" He told me that instead of sitting around a large table eating and drinking, they had found inspiration in Western films and went on to create an evening that was a mixture of a traditional Chinese party with karaoke, and a Western one with disco, costumes and games. I suddenly realized that the party goers I had seen running around blowing tooters in the lobby late the night before as I was checking in were the same well-behaved network managers that I had just given a lecture to.

It would have been improbable a few years ago for business creativity to be the highlight of a conference for local telecoms managers at a large state-owned Chinese company in a medium-sized Chinese town. But these days it is quite normal. Just as normal as teaching the same managers how to relax by organizing a party with tooters and party hats. Wild parties probably do not prove it is wrong to say that Asians cannot be creative because they are frightened of losing face. After all, a few fun parties do not change traditions that are thousands of years old. However, they do show that Asians are becoming less constrained and more creative.

One evening in Beijing, I found myself on a stage doing improvisation theatre. Ten of the thirty participants were there for the first time. Just like ripples on water, news spread about a new way of thinking freely. And even though some of the participants were a bit stiff when it came to improvising, it was wonderful to see how they blossomed during the evening and became more and more daring. As I watched a petite Chinese woman playing the role of a sexually excited nurse who inflicted wounds on patients because she liked to see blood, it struck me how these small occurrences were signs that people's thoughts were changing slowly but surely.

Put the millions of small changes at grassroots level together, and see how those who have created these changes talk about them with their partners, colleagues and siblings, who in their turn, are then inspired to question why their employer, university or association cannot do the same thing – and it soon becomes clear that greater changes are on the way, even if we cannot detect them yet.

Professor Ron Newman at Raffles University is another person who has witnessed the results of the development of creative studies in China. Raffles is a private design and business college founded by Chew Hua Seng in Singapore. They held their first design course in China in 1990. That first year they had twenty students, of which fifteen quit because they did not understand English. At the end of that year, there were more teachers than students in the college. Since then, however, China and the rest of Asia have seen a dramatic increase in people interested in design courses. Within five years, Raffles predicts that it will have more than 150,000 students in its different colleges around Asia. The rapid expansion of educational companies like Raffles means that there is an increasingly large number of graduates within the creative industries. These graduates are sorely needed because of the demand for people with these particular skills.

The rising popularity of the so-called creative industries, which has ensured the success of companies like Raffles, is also changing the face of other educational institutes in developing countries.

Mr. Lin manages MBA courses at Xiamen University in China. The university was founded back in 1921 and was the first university to offer MBA courses. Not surprisingly, the university has China's third best management course. When the university first started its EMBA course (Executive Masters of Business Administration), companies would ask for the creativity components of the course to be left out as they just did not see the point of having them. But something happened a few years ago.

When China first opened its doors to enterprises, they did not need to innovate. It was enough to take a Western product or business and establish an equivalent one in China. Those times are now over. In a recent survey, the university asked its graduates what stopped them from starting up their own businesses. They did not say that the lack of money, resources or contacts was the problem. The most common answer was the lack of business possibilities. The Chinese have suddenly begun to realize that it is not sufficient merely to find a hole and fill it; they have to start making their own holes and be creative. The result? The courses in creativity and innovation are among the most popular.

The more I have travelled around the developing world, the clearer it becomes that there is a creative grassroots revolution. And the more obvious it becomes, the more difficult it is to understand why we thought it could never happen. Joachim Rosenberg is responsible for Volvo Trucks in Asia and has worked in both developed and developing countries. He does not believe that the creative revolution at grassroots level is an illusion. "We mocked the Japanese and we sniggered at the Koreans, and now we are laughing at the Chinese. How many Chinese cars did we see at Frankfurt three years ago? How many exhibit there today? And how many will there be in three years' time?"

The answer I got from two young Turkish designers whom I interviewed in Istanbul was perhaps the clearest and the loudest. I asked them why relatively few people in developed countries fully understood the extent of the creative transformation going on in countries like Turkey. They said that it was because we were too busy remembering the head start we used to have instead of getting out there and seizing all the possibilities that are being created right now. Or as they put it, **"It's like when a girl breaks up with her boyfriend. The old boyfriend keeps thinking about her when he should be out looking for a new girl instead."**

The results of this creative revolution may not be fully visible at the moment. But if we choose to see a change only when everything has been revolutionized, then we will find ourselves lagging behind. This is a lesson that many have learnt throughout history – for example, at the end of the twentieth century when the Internet made its breakthrough.

The IT **revolution** of our era

My first encounter with the Internet took place in the beginning of 1994. My girlfriend at that time was studying in the USA and I was in Sweden. It was too expensive to call and letters took a long time to be delivered. Then I heard that there was a way of sending 'electronic letters' via a computer, so I talked my way into the Computer Club of The Royal Institute of Technology even though I was not a student there. As I wrote my first e-mail, the more experienced students showed me the World Wide Web for the very first time. I still remember the incredible feeling of playing chess in real time against someone in the US. That was when I realized that the Internet would be a major revolution. I established a web-consulting agency during the second half of the 1990s and found myself right in the middle of the dot-com boom. During those years, I gave a lot of lectures about the nature of the Internet, which allowed me to see how it went from being an insignificant plaything for nerds to an interesting tool for many. Nowadays we take the Internet for granted; but fifteen years ago, it was insignificant, irrelevant and virtually unknown.

The creative changes going on in the developing world today remind me of the Internet revolution of earlier years. The Internet had existed in different guises for decades before it made a breakthrough. Suddenly, in the middle of the 1990s, the time was right for the Internet explosion. And in just a few years, more developments had occurred than even the experts had dreamed of. Nearly everybody working with the Internet was surprised by how quickly the changes occurred. We were also astonished by the fact that most people were indifferent to the revolution we thought the world was undergoing. James Seng is a Singaporean pioneer, who started an Internet company back in 1993. He also helped establish one of Singapore's first Internet service providers. He has worked in his own Internet company as well as being an advisor to the Singaporean government in the telecoms and Internet arenas. Nowadays, he is a partner of Thymos Capital, which invests in Internet start-ups in Singapore, Cambodia and China. Over tea in the bar of the classic Raffles Hotel in Singapore, we discussed the similarities between the Internet boom of the 1990s and the expansion of creativity going on in developing countries. According to James, a lot of people in the developed world are making the same mistakes that many companies did when they were evaluating the Internet. "A lot of people from developed countries come to the developing world wearing their 'developed country glasses'. They compare what we are doing with the way things are done back home and exclaim, "This sucks!" The small number of web sites and Internet users that existed in 1995 did not seem to be significant or earth shattering. In much the same way, it is dangerous to look at what is going on in developing countries when it comes to creativity and dismiss it as being irrelevant. This is James' advice to us: **"Flip it around and look at things from a different perspective. Don't judge the developing world on where it is today – but on how far it has come during the past couple of years.** Ask yourselves, 'Where will they be in five years from now if this fast pace continues?' I think a lot of companies will be scared by the conclusions they draw." In 1998, Google was a new and small company that you would never have considered to be a threat to a giant like Microsoft. Ten years on and Google dominates the business. As it turned out, not that many established companies went out of business because they did not jump on the Internet bandwagon, so the risks facing the developed world now should not be exaggerated. However, the risk of going out of business is not really relevant here. Just as the established companies missed out on a great chance by not realizing the relevance of the Internet, so too is the developed world missing out on the possibilities that are available or being created in developing countries.

If we, the developed world, want to take full advantage of what is going on in the world today, then we will have to be a lot better at noticing changes, understanding their implications and implementing them more quickly. Perhaps there is a lesson to learn from those well-established institutions: they could have learnt so much – and understood what was happening – by just listening to the young, dynamic Internet companies of the 1990s.

In much the same way, we would benefit if we could let go of our prestige and become better at listening to what the people in developing countries have to teach us about the world right now.

The most common objection to my thesis that the most exciting ideas and innovations are going to come from developing countries is this: "If it's going to happen then why don't we see more companies like Apple and Google in India and China?"

People in developing countries have a good answer: "Wait and see!"

Five to **ten years**

The changes that we can see in the developing world have gathered momentum over the past five to ten years, and right now, we are in the middle of it all. Or to quote the HR Manager of Sina.com, Arthur Duan, who put it like this: "We have spent that last twenty years catching up. We'll be spending the next twenty overtaking. Just give China another five to ten years."

When I ask people in developing countries how long it is going to take before we can really see the big changes, I nearly always hear the same reply, "In five to ten years." Most people say this with frustration as if this were just too long; as if they hoped, and even believed, that it could happen sooner. This frustration about catching up (and overtaking) surprised me in the beginning – until I realised the huge changes that have already occurred over the past five to ten years.

Let's look at the Indian fashion industry. It did not exist – in modern terms – ten years ago. Then the fashion business just exploded. The Indian fashion designer Narenda Kumar believes that we will soon talk about Mumbai in the same breath as New York or Paris when it comes to fashion. "The change that has taken place during the past ten years is truly remarkable. My country has – literally – changed dramatically before my very eyes during the last five to eight years. These changes took decades in developed countries, while here in India, we are talking in terms of years." The Indian designers Aparna and Norden Wangdi agreed when I asked them if we are soon going to see an 'Indian Gucci'. "Yes. This could happen in the next four to five years, or it could take ten to fifteen. We have been living in Delhi for twenty years now, and a whole new city has taken shape before our eyes in the last five to eight years. We never thought things would change so rapidly. We have international brands, and we have shopping malls, which did not exist here before. Considering the speed at which these changes are occurring, it is just a matter of time before we have our own strong global brands." These rapid and powerful changes in recent years have had a big impact on creative entrepreneurs. "It's great. We can really see the changes and this means that we are getting our act together. It's forcing us to become faster, better, more competitive – and more creative too. Our brains are working overtime. We're very lucky to be in India right now."

You could say that developing countries have moved up a gear in order to start competing seriously with developed nations in the creative arenas. This rapid development can be seen not only in the fashion industry in India, but also in the property business in China and the computer industry in Singapore. Yee-Chia Yeo, Assistant Professor at the Department of Electrical and Computer Engineering at the National University of Singapore, leads research in the field of semiconductor technology and nano-sized transistors. He too has noticed how Singapore has changed over the past few years. After his studies in the USA, he moved back to Singapore. **"There is momentum here – I can feel it. It makes more sense for me to stay here than move. I just had to come back – and I did so gladly – because there are so many opportunities here right now."**

When I asked him why he thought more people had not noticed this change, he said it was because people who are not experts tend to simplify certain subjects and this is why it takes longer for them to notice changes. He gives the world of fashion as an example. He is leading nanotechnologist; not a fashion expert, so he assumes that French fashion is the best there is. And although fashion experts have noticed that new cities are now competing on this front with Paris, it is not something that Yee-Chia Yeo, an amateur, can see. So it is within his own area of expertise. Most people know nothing about the latest advances in nanotechnology, so they might assume that the most exciting research being done in this high-tech area is being carried out in the States, whereas, in fact, advances are being made in Asia too. When I once asked a Malaysian creative what message she wanted to send back to the people in developed countries who do not think that the change in developing countries will happen so quickly she looked me straight in the eyes and said: "You underestimate the Asians and overestimate yourself." Then she smiled and added: "Overconfidence is bad."

The experienced Swedish entrepreneur Jan Staël von Holstein has seen these creative melting pots before. He moved with the creative revolution in the West, from New York in the 1960s and 70s, via Italy to London when the revolution reached Europe. Now, at 60, he lives part-time in Shanghai because he wants to follow the creative development in China at close quarters. "The next creative revolution is going to happen in Shanghai or Beijing," he claims. "In five or ten years' time, history will repeat itself and in the future we will look back and see that sometime between 2010 and 2020 something new was created in Shanghai. It is impossible to say what it will be. It could be a new art form, an innovative technology or a new philosophy. We do not know what it will be - but it will blow us away." Perhaps it is this feeling of uncertainty about what is going to happen – while at the same time being 100% convinced that something is going to occur – that I find so appealing. The really major breakthroughs in history happen in such big steps that those who are alive while they are going on do not even notice the changes. According to Jan Staël von Holstein, we are living in such an era now. And I fully agree with him.

If you want to know what the world might be like, then South Korea is an interesting example.

South Korea - The future is already here

Soong Yee Yoon works at SK Telecom, South Korea's largest mobile operator. According to her, **Korea is neither a developed nor a developing country: it is a dynamic country.**

This is a good name to put on a country, I think, because South Korea is a country that refuses to let itself become 'developed', that refuses to stand still. So, in spite of the fact that the country is the world's tenth largest economy and a member of the OECD, and has an average wage that is 30% higher than that of Sweden, it still does not want to define itself as a developed country. It is not ready to declare that it is complete because people believe that their country can become even better than it already is. Full speed ahead is the name of the game.

Korea's modern design history is only 20 years old. Hyoung-Bae Kim has been part of it since the start. Mr. Kim is 47 years old and has spent 12 years as a designer at Samsung. However, now he has left and started up his own company. His new title is President and CEO and his company is called S-cluster. It is a small, creative industry design company that has won international prizes for its products. When he was a young student, he – literally – studied by candlelight. As South Korea has gone from being a poor, underdeveloped country to a rich and successful one in just one generation, he believes that this is why people still have the desire to develop. They can remember when they were worse off. We had this desire in the West as well, up to the 1960s perhaps, but it has more or less worn off now that we have begun to think of ourselves as developed.

While I was in South Korea, I also met Steve Bowen, director at the PR company Edelman. Originally from England, he has lived in Korea for more than fourteen years. Once, he and a 55-year-old Korean friend, visited a traditional Korean house with an earthen floor, and his friend told him that he had grown up in a house like this. It is when you hear stories like this that you realize just how fast South Korea has developed. However, I believe that very few Westerners understand just how quickly things are changing.

I must admit that I was impressed by how far the South Koreans have come. They have had mobile TV for years. They can use their cell phones to pay in shops. They are number one in the world when it comes to being connected via broadband and they have developed their economy faster than all the other major economies during the past 30 years. Yet they still refuse to say that they are fully developed.

"We don't regard ourselves as number one. Because when you are number one, there is nowhere else to go. Nothing else to develop. It is when you are number two, when you have something to fight for, that you move forwards," a manager told me when I expressed my amazement about how much South Korea had developed during the 20 years that have passed since my last visit there.

Tarras Delin is in charge of the Swedish Trade Council in South Korea. He shares my astonishment about how the Koreans are not satisfied with everything they have already achieved. "Korea sees itself as Japan's little brother and will never be happy until it has overtaken Japan. At the same time, the Koreans can feel China breathing down their necks – so this has also led to their realization that they can't stand still. They still view themselves as small shrimp squeezed between the two whales that are China and Japan." The result? A steadily increasing stream of creativity. The South Korean wave has already washed over Asia: South Korean soap operas are extremely popular in China and Singapore; the singer Rain is a hit in Asia and the girls go crazy when he visits Bangkok. According to Delin, Chinese women go to South Korea for plastic surgery. This is in itself is nothing new as they have been doing so for many years. However, before, they wanted to look Western; nowadays, they want to look Korean. This is, of course, due in part to the fact that it is easier to make a Chinese look Korean. However, it also goes to show that South Korea has succeeded in creating an image of itself as a cool, modern and trend-setting country. Up until now, these trends have mainly reached other Asian countries – not because the Koreans lack creativity, but because of our lack of interest in trends from the East.

Lars Vargö, the Swedish ambassador in South Korea, used to be ambassador in Japan when it was one of the fastest developing countries in the world. He can see the similarities between Japan back then and

73

the South Korea of today: that same joy in life that he noted in Japan in 1977 is prevalent in Korea. It has the same positive attitude and enthusiasm about what it wants to achieve. When I asked him what we in the West could learn from the Koreans, he said urgently, **"We have to dare to think new thoughts. As things stand at the moment, our thoughts are stunted. We have exchanged outdated norms for ones that are too narrow."**

The developed world is stuck in a narrow rut while South Korea continues to question how things have been, are being and should be done. I hear this over and over again from nearly everyone I meet in South Korea.

I left South Korea and landed in Europe with a mixture of fear and joy. I was happy about the overwhelming positive energy that I had seen in South Korea, and scared about the lack of acceptance of change in the part of the world I was arriving in.

I felt as if I had reached a different world, and I remembered my meeting a few weeks before in China with a senior manager of one of Sweden's most successful corporations. He told me about a visit he had received from a delegation of Swedish members of Parliament. He asked the politicians what they thought they could learn from the Chinese. The politicians laughed and said, "Don't you mean what the Chinese can learn from us?"

THEIR
ADVANTAGES

How those living in **developing countries have** a number of **advantages** when it comes to making the most of the changes that are happening in the world, as well as a look at what those advantages are and what they mean.

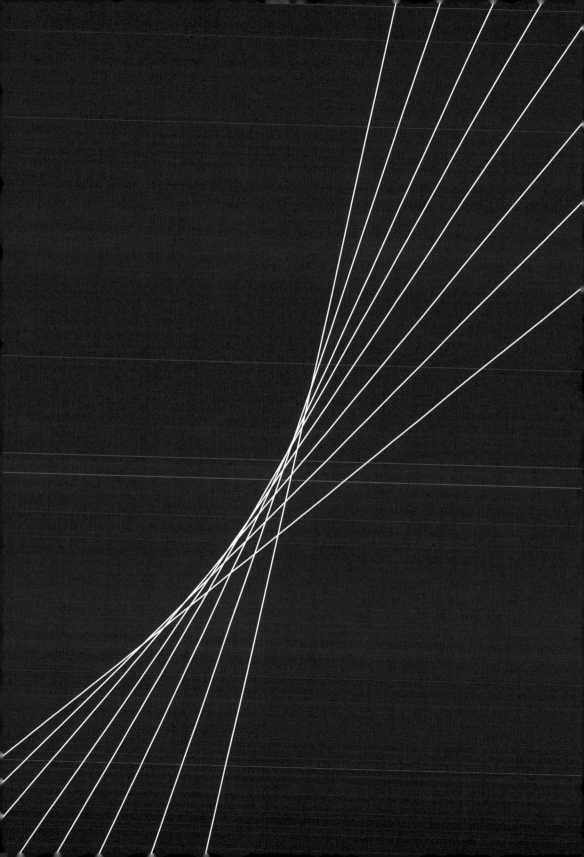

The Developing **Dream**

The Indian fashion business is a good starting point if you want to understand the changes that are happening in developing countries. And if you want to understand the fashion business in India, then Narendra Kumar is the right person to interview. He has been involved in the fashion scene in India for nearly as long as it has existed. He started India's first fashion magazine in 1996, Elle India. As well as designing clothes under several of his own labels, he has worked as a consultant for international fashion brands, including Levis when they wanted help to get established in India. "You cannot work in the fashion industry unless you understand and embrace change. And right now it is essential to understand just how fast this market is changing. The younger generation here has a sense of urgency. They want to learn, achieve and search for the new. **"One of our strong points is that our thoughts are not limited as they are in the developed world. And because we are constantly developing, we have fewer limits when it comes to thinking – so we can think more freely. I'm convinced that this allows us to think more broadly and deeply than you can in a world that considers itself to be fully developed."**

Narendra believes that this feeling of having no boundaries affects the way people think in India, no matter whether it is about architecture or fashion, culture or business. According to him, this open way of looking at the future is new; and although you might think that this unwillingness to limit oneself, while also daring to have bigger and freer dreams, is a little naïve, Narendra is fully aware that not all dreams come true. That is why they are called dreams. "There is a kind of intoxication here. Now is the time to think big. We're ready to bulldoze our way into the world today. There will be successes and failures, but that is a natural part of dreaming." Of course, just dreaming does not create change. Narendra says that there has been more than a dramatic increase in dreams during the past few years. It has also become easier to make these dreams come true, which is just as important. For example, it is easier to find financing for your ideas as more and more people believe that new ideas can, in fact, generate money.

More dreams. Bigger dreams. Easier to make them a reality. More and more people deciding to implement their dreams. Everything happening at the same time. Narendra says that the result is a magical feeling of being able to do things. **"In India today we are in awe of what we can achieve. We are amazed by what we have already done and by what we can do in the future. You can feel the energy in the streets – you can almost touch it. Suddenly, people are realizing that ideas can be turned into great things and dreams can come true."** If more and more people have greater dreams and everyone can see that an increasing number of these dreams are coming true, then a lot of energy is created. This energy, in turn, creates more hope and belief in the future. It is not only new products and services that are being developed in developing countries – people are too. And their dreams. Narendra concludes our conversation. "In India, you wake up and think about what you can achieve today." How often do feel like this when you wake up in the mornings?

When I was invited to speak at Design Week KL in Malaysia in 2010 I got to hear a speech from YB Dato Mukhriz Mahathir, Deputy Minister of International Trade and Industry in Malaysia. In his passionate speech he talked about the need for creative people in Malaysia to dare to dream and what those dreams could lead to. He said: "When things come together for you, when you start realising your dreams, you'll also begin to make other´s dreams come true."

In a world where people feel that anything is possible, then nearly everything is possible. In a world where people feel that most things have already been done, then not much is done. This does not mean that there are no dreams in developed countries, or that all dreams in developing countries come true. One advantage that the inhabitants of developing countries have is that in their world it is easier to have great dreams and to believe that they will become a reality. In a world that believes most things are yet to be done, then the possibilities there feel endless and obtainable. Or to quote Ingvar Kamprad, the founder of IKEA: "Most things still remain to be done. The future is glorious!"

Having big dreams is an advantage. But it takes more than just dreams to create advancement. Paradoxically, the fact that we think we have an advantage in the developing world may turn out to be an advantage for the developing world.

Not stuck in old infrastructure

Dialog Telekom is a mobile operator in Sri Lanka, a developing country with a mobile penetration of just over 30%. Dialog produced an SMS dating service, which they then turned into a blood donation service when the country suffered a dengue fever epidemic. This service won a 'GSM Oscar' for best innovative community service. The company has also launched a new life insurance service for five rupees a month that can be paid for via debit card. The life insurance is a service for those who are too poor to get insurance on an annual basis. The idea is that they can get insurance cover for the months they have paid for. Dialog's slogan is 'The Future. Today.' A slogan that is really fitting. Dialog may well be a mobile operator in the poor and war-stricken country of Sri Lanka, yet it is still a very innovative company. For example, it was one of the first in the world to offer a payment solution between customers and shops.

Ravi Abeysekera is in charge of Dialog's mobile bank services. He believes that there are several reasons why a mobile operator in a developing country like Sri Lanka can develop more quickly than big operators in developed countries. **"When two mature giants try to be innovative, it isn't easy."** He argues that major established players on a mature market can find it difficult to find fast, effective ways of collaborating due to their size and slowness.

However, Ravi thinks that the main reason for mobile payment solutions being launched in developing countries instead of developed ones is that the users in these countries are not mentally or physically stuck in the old infrastructure. Payment services via your mobile have been around in countries like South Africa, the Philippines and Bangladesh for years. Even the financially disastrous country of Zimbabwe has services that allow you to pay via a cell phone. India was the first country in the world to carry out a major test where customers could even transfer money from one country to another using their mobile phones. Meanwhile, in developed countries, it is often still not possible to transfer money between two cell phones. How can it be possible in India but not in, say, Sweden? The answer lies partly in the old infrastructure – or, should I say, in the lack of infrastructure. Very few shops in Sri Lanka have credit card readers and very few Sri Lankans have credit cards - yet many of them have mobile phones – so it was easier for Dialog to change their customers' behaviour. You could say that, in this case, the lack of infrastructure made it possible to create a new one.

Infrastructure is not necessarily just physical: an organization can be stuck in a mental rut too. By establishing a certain way of doing things that seems to work, there is a risk that you also set a working method in stone and miss a better way of doing things. A mental infrastructure is treacherous in that it is difficult to identify, thus making it difficult to know what rut you are stuck in. It is even more perfidious when you think that you are doing something in the best way possible.

Let me give you an example: due to my extensive travels, I have had the chance to see how the mental infrastructure about how an airport should be managed has developed more rapidly in the developing world than in the developed one during the past few years. I landed at the airport in Colombo, Sri Lanka, at the beginning of 2008, and when I disembarked, I realized that five years had gone by since my very first visit. Going through passport control, I noticed that quite a few things had quietly changed over these five years. The first time I visited Sri Lanka, I had to stand in line for an hour to show my passport. Now – five years later – I waited three minutes. I have been to Sri Lanka six times over the past year and have never had to wait for more than three minutes.

Once, when I landed at Mumbai, I thought to myself: "Indian red tape has got such a bad reputation! I'll probably have to stand and queue for hours." Much to my surprise, there was no queue at all. In fact, I was so astonished that I went up to the person in charge of passport control at Mumbai Airport and praised the service I had just experienced. He smiled and said, **"Thanks. We like to try out innovative ways of making life easier for our passengers."**

You know things are happening out there in the world – or at least in parts of the world – when an Indian passport control officer starts talking about innovative ways of improving service! I still hear how

81

people have to wait for hours to get through security and passport control at Heathrow Airport in London. It has become a bit better during the past year or so, but services have not improved at the same speed or level as those in Sri Lanka have, for example.

So – faster, more innovative and service-centred improvements at airports in Sri Lanka and India. No big improvements in London. A small, yet significant, example of how developing countries are developing faster than developed ones these days, and how they are not stuck in a mental infrastructure about how things 'should' be done. If you look closely, you can see all sorts of small, quiet changes going on in the developing world.

Another new solution that you can find in Sri Lanka is that you ring just one number no matter which public official you want to reach. An operator connects you to the correct person. In South Korea, you can find petrol pumps hanging from the roof of the petrol filling station so that there are no big pumps in the way when you want to fill up your car. Steve Bowen from the consultancy firm Edelman says that Koreans and others living in developing nations find it easier to develop new products and services than those in developed countries because they are mentally more flexible. "Their mental infrastructure is still developing," is how he puts it.

According to the Indian professor Amarnath, developing countries do not suffer from the classic 'not invented here' mentality because they have not yet invented that much. This kind of mentality means refusing to bring in good ideas from outside in the belief that you are better at finding your own solutions. **Developing countries, however, have the more positive mentality of 'not YET invented here'.** This way of thinking allows you to absorb other people's ideas and be inspired by their solutions while waiting to come up with your own improved solutions. Professor Amarnath declared that our future is controlled by our past and he went on to explain that India is not stuck in a rut when it comes to thinking about how new technology can be used. He calls this the 'No Memory Effect' – by not following old patterns of thinking it is easier to see new things with fresh eyes.

By defining ourselves as leading the pack, we get stuck in our current ways and are thus limited in our search for new solutions. Saying that we have an advantage is not the same thing as actually having one. Many of those living in developed countries are stuck with the same old tools that they think are modern. At the same time, many people in developing countries use the latest technology while considering themselves to be upstarts, who must work even harder.

Learning from those in the lead

A few years back at an international conference in Stockholm the moderator introduced Abhilasha Hans, Customer Service Manager at the Indian mobile operator Airtel, with the following words: "Give a warm round of applause to Abhilasha Hans, Customer Service Manager of a company that gets a million new customers per month." When she got up on stage, Abhilasha modestly corrected the moderator, "Thanks. I'd just like to start off with one small correction: we don't get one million new customers per month. We get two." The audience laughed and, as I stood there in the wings, I got goosebumps. Just imagine: a company that month after month gets two million new customers!

Abhilasha is passionately interested in creativity and new ideas. She told me that business creativity is essential in order to develop at such a furious pace. One of the difficulties customer services in India experience is the fact that there are so many official languages. When customers call, personnel must be able to answer questions in the right language. Actually the 15 official languages are not the greatest problem – it is the 325 different dialects.

Airtel is an interesting company in many ways. It is the fastest growing mobile operator, going from 0 to 50 million customers. They are not India's first mobile operator; they started up relatively late. They decided to turn to their advantage the fact that other mobile operators already existed around the world and so they looked at how you should – and should not – run such a company. One conclusion they came to was that a good way of growing rapidly and profitably was to outsource a large part of their business. An innovative company like Airtel has made the most of this. Most of their business is based on services they buy: for example, IBM is in charge of all their IT. Instead of buying mobile transmitters, switchboards and other technology, they hire these services from Ericsson. For strategic reasons, Airtel has its own research and development departments.

Airtel can offer services that do not exist in Europe. Yet, Abhilasha told me that it is highly unusual for European mobile operators to

visit them in India in order to see if they can learn anything from a company that attracts one or two million customers a month.

It is even rarer for American operators to contact them and ask if they can visit. It just does not happen. As for the visiting Europeans, they come mainly from Eastern Europe. Abhilasha does not react to the fact that so few Western companies want to learn from Airtel. She is used to it. Nor does she reflect over how obvious it is to her (as an employee of a developing company) that she should travel and check out new services in the West. **It is this very curiosity about the world that makes a company like Airtel an innovative one, and it is this curiosity that makes innovative companies so strong. The lack of this curiosity is the weakest point of many Western companies.**

One reason for visiting developing countries is that they have come further than we have. Indeed, some claim that the world's most sophisticated consumers can be found in the developing world.

Sophisticated Chinese

Djamal Farroug is the director of Planet Caviar in the trendy district of Xintiandi in Shanghai. Planet Caviar sells what is best described as extreme premium food, as it sells only Russian caviar, Alaskan crab, champagne and expensive wines. Some of the most expensive bottles of wine cost about 1,500 Euro. Caviar costs from 1,200 EUR for 30 grams up to 10,000 EUR for 500 grams. After ten years in Geneva, Planet Caviar opened its second store in Shanghai, with a third one due to open in Hong Kong and a fourth in Beijing. There are no plans to expand in cities of the developed world like Paris, London or New York. The newly opened shop in Shanghai is doing booming business. As Djamal, the man who runs the shop, says, "It's crazy. Simply crazy. And in the future, it will be even crazier. The Chinese really know how to spend money, and now that they have a lot of it, they spend a lot too." He continues: "The market is here. The people who have money are in this part of the world. There are a lot of rich people in China nowadays and they like to spend."

China will soon be the world's largest market for luxury products. And though you could accuse the Chinese of having money but not taste a few years ago, even this has changed quickly. **"These days customers know what they want. And why,"** Djamal told me.

It is easy to believe that markets in developing countries are less sophisticated than those in the developed world – but this attitude can be dangerous. In many areas, the opposite is true. Africa has the highest percentage of people who surf the Internet via mobile phones. The Chinese manager of IKEA had to call home to Sweden to ask them to remove the adverts for TV benches from the Chinese catalogue as the Chinese either do not have TV or hang their flat screen TVs on the wall. The Chinese consumer is also advanced when it comes to brands. Pete Heskett is Head of Planning at the international advertising agency BBH in Shanghai. This is what he has to say: "Chinese consumers are very modern when it comes to relating to brands. They are into brands in the plural, but are less loyal to specific ones. So, they switch brands quite often. If we take alcohol as an example: they will be drinking Johnnie Walker one month; Chivas the next;

and then they will move onto vodka. They have this constant cycle of trying out new stuff. They are not loyal, which I think is a very sophisticated and modern way of relating to brands."

According to Pete, people in developed countries say that they are, for example, 'Nokia people' – meaning that they can only imagine using a Nokia cell phone. Pete believes that this is a dreary way of looking at brands. A Chinese is much more likely to test different brands. However – and this is an important point – they are only willing to test other brands that are as good. This makes the Chinese market a tough one when it comes to marketing. As brand manager of a company you have to make sure you have a strong brand while also accepting the fact that customers will be disloyal and go to your competitors too. This is why you can see very aggressive marketing campaigns for perfume and other luxury items in cities like Shanghai and Beijing. Companies have to work hard all the time to ensure that customers buy their products. When Pete says that the Chinese only choose among different well-known brands, it is important to understand that he does not mean that they act like angst-ridden teenagers who always follow the latest trend. What he means is that it is the curiosity of the Chinese consumers when it comes to different good brands that prompts them to try out different things. They experiment with different roles instead of limiting themselves to being a certain type of person or customer. You could say that the consumer is less like a 40-year-old hard rock fan who still wears his Iron Maiden T-shirt and more like Madonna who experiments with different styles: sometimes following trends; sometimes making them. When I asked Pete how he thought that the people at home in the West would react if he told them that Chinese consumers are more sophisticated and modern than their Western counterparts, he began to laugh. "Why – they'd probably look at me and wonder if I'd been smoking crack! That's how unaware people at home are about what's going on over here," he replied. Of course, Pete has not been smoking crack: he has just travelled from the West to Shanghai and understood something that most of us have not grasped fully yet: the consumers that have developed most in the developing world are more advanced than consumers in the West.

Paradoxically, developing countries use newer, more advanced solutions than we do while also feeling that they are lagging behind, thus working harder to keep up. We can see similar paradoxes when it comes to feeling like an underdog in the business arena. IKEA is viewed as both an upstart and the world's leading furniture company. Google still has that aura of being an underdog in spite of the fact that it is ten years old and a giant that everyone wants to beat.

While the people in the developing world can be some of the most sophisticated customers in the world, they can still think of themselves as country bumpkins. This drives them to fight their way forward with even more zeal.

Freedom equals **possibility**

"Over the years of interviewing people, I have been struck by how many of them – at the top of their professions – come from small towns. And I think that many of these people, who have been so determined to get away from those towns, then go on to use this grit to become successful. Their passion helps them get far. I think that this phenomenon can also be seen in developing countries. We are the country hicks of the world – and this makes us even more determined to exceed expectations and do better than anybody thought possible." The woman who compares people from developing countries to the inhabitants of the world's small towns is Pnina Fenster. As editor of Glamour magazine in South Africa, she has a finger in many creative pies. Naturally, she is a part of the fashion scene since she is the editor of a fashion magazine, but she is also at home in the art and music scenes as well as having contacts in the graphic design and advertising businesses. She is passionate about creativity – and, above all, about helping people find a way of expressing it.

You can find her office in a building right in the middle of one of Cape Town's many hills. Table Top Mountain rises majestically in the background and at the foot of the hill, you can see the ocean. She wonders rhetorically how it is possible not to be creative amid such beauty. Although the beauty of Cape Town and the rest of South Africa is fuel for creativity, she does not want to acknowledge nature for the creative revolution going on in South Africa right now. Instead, she points to Robben Island, where Nelson Mandela spent a large part of his 27 years in prison.

"There is no question that democracy took a lid off things and just allowed all kinds of elements to bubble up and flower – and also take root. Democracy opened up opportunities and mindsets. And creativity is a mindset. **We went from a very narrow, fascist mindset, which affected and damaged everybody, to a democratic mindset and the feeling that everything is possible. In a country where a political prisoner who spent nearly 30 years in jail can become president we have created the feeling that nothing is impossible. This feeling has led to a huge burst of energy."**

This new-found freedom has boosted the creative confidence of the South Africans. "We went from being incredibly oppressed – just over a decade ago – to suddenly seeing the world open up to us. This has created an incredible feeling of can-do in the country."

South Africa has scampered onto the creative scene like a young springbok in the first green pasture of spring – even if its legs are still a bit wobbly. Pnina told me that sometimes all this creative freedom has been channelled ineffectively and she is well aware of the new problems that arise in a young democracy that finds itself in the middle of a fast-paced development. She is also aware that the country has many old problems to solve: everything from poverty to AIDS. She pointed out that in spite of this she believes that, on the whole, something positive and new is being created. **"I think we are fresher; we have a new kind of enthusiasm, a naïve feeling of freedom that means we are not as limited as you are. The developed world, the West, has become so blasé."**

While the developed world tries to create saleable products and global concepts, many people in countries like South Africa are busy creating for the sake of creating. I asked Pnina to explain what the advantages are of their view on creativity, and it strikes me that the feeling she describes is what propels fashion designers to travel around the world looking for the latest trends in urban fashion. They want to find something fresh, created out of passion, curiosity and love - not primarily done to make money. Over-commercialized products like the TV programme Idol will always sell. But those that are created from the heart will go deeper because they are real. It is this feeling of being genuine that Pnina sees in creative people in developing countries.

Naturally, it takes more than creative energy to create global success. You need knowledge about marketing, international trends, professionalism and other qualities to create a leading fashion organization – and this kind of knowledge did not exist before in countries like South Africa, but a lot has happened in this area over the past few years. For example, Fashion Week has only existed in Africa for about ten years. There is a thirst there to learn how to show the world way what you have created, and to do that in a professional way. Pnina told me that they have now left behind a system that suffocated creativity – partly because of a limiting oppressive political situation, and partly because they did not have a structure which could turn ideas into innovations. When the political oppression stopped, a period of creative chaos followed, in which the new-found political freedom gave people the feeling of total creative freedom. Many of the ideas that arose at this time were too free in expression to be turned into commercial successes. They are now at the point where creative expression is liberating but controlled enough to be able to turn ideas into something useful.

I think of that young springbok again: how it rushes out into the green fields a little too fast and uncontrolled at first. Before it manages to get its legs under control, it has fallen over a couple of times. Then it grows into an animal full of energy and power. I do not know what Pnina would think of my metaphor; but I think she would approve. I have come across this same creative, positive feeling of possibility in many Eastern European countries that have broken free from the constraints of being a part of a closed Soviet Union to create a freer political system. The feeling of liberation has become much greater in many of these countries during recent years. After an era of economic and political chaos, they are finally glimpsing new opportunities. They are allowed to do more – and they can do more. They want to do more – and they dare do it too.

I asked Pnina what happens when you combine that heady feeling of freedom about being able to do what you want with the feeling that you want to achieve things just because you can and then pair them up with the knowledge of the demands the international market places on them.

"Well, hopefully, if you add all of that together, you get creative dynamite – in the best possible way," she said confidently and with a big smile on her face.

Do people in developed countries take their freedom for granted? Does this result in us not appreciating and understanding how this freedom can give us the energy to create new things? Just as we sometimes cannot see the tree for the trees, perhaps the will to use creative freedom is stronger in those who have only just realized that their freedom has increased. Is it at all possible for the people in the developed world to regain that positive feeling that Pnina describes? How can we create creative dynamite? My sheltered Swedish soul reacted when I wrote the words 'creative dynamite'. Can you use such an expression? Isn't dynamite a bit too dangerous? Then I realized that I was suffering from that need-for-security virus that strikes down the developed person. A virus that makes us too cautious – and that might well make us too afraid to take risks.

Dare to take risks

Padmaja Ruparel is one of the driving forces behind the Indian Angel Network, an organization that brings together a large number of business 'angels' – that is, successful entrepreneurs from India and around the world who are interested in investing in start up's and newly started businesses. **She has noticed the fear that exists in the developed world - the fear that something might go wrong. She is convinced that we put too much energy into trying to predict what might go wrong, and then spending even more energy and resources on trying to minimize the risk of something negative happening.** Naturally, we should try to prevent bad things from happening, but we should also realize that it is impossible to be sheltered from everything. "It's the same thing as when your raise a child. You can protect your child but you can't protect her too much – otherwise, she will become too vulnerable."

Richard Hassell from the prize-winning design firm WoHa in Singapore agrees with Padmaja. Raised in Australia, he has worked for many years in Singapore. His company has completed building projects in Australia and Singapore and he can compare attitudes to his company's ideas in both developed Australia and developing Singapore."We have a project in Sydney that I find immensely limiting and negative. The reason for this is that the customer is afraid of taking risks. Every time we come up with an idea, we always get a negative comment about why it won't work. So the immediate response is not to get excited about a new idea, but to see it as a problem." He told me about the time they had suggested that the Australian clients put palm trees on the roof of a skyscraper. Their spontaneous reaction was not that this idea was interesting or good: "The risk of palm leaves blowing off and hitting someone's car was more horrifying than the delight you would get from seeing palm trees on the roof." When WoHa suggested that the leaves could be pruned so that they did not blow off, the reaction was fear that the leaves would not be cut back in time. This attitude is a good reflection of the kind of attitude many customers in the developed world have. "What we in the developed world are saying by this is that the value of a safe and completely sanitized environment is higher than the joy and excitement you get from innovation and experimentation. What we are saying is, in effect, that the risks outweigh the benefits."

In the developing world, people try to manage risks, while in the developed world we try to minimize them. Richard says that we have lost the ability to take risks as we are just too afraid; paralyzed by a fear of the future, of things going wrong; and by the fear of losing what we already have. In a world that is obsessed by trying to identify and minimize risks, there is an even greater risk that you are making the mistake of focusing on the wrong things. You put a lot of energy and resources into trying to fix things that do not need fixing purely out of the fear of being criticized should something go wrong. The main problem with this is that there is no time or resources left for more important things.

Sometimes the fear of making a mistake can lead to comical results. Due to its tough indemnity laws, the USA has turned into one of the most extreme examples of how much effort organizations and corporations put into minimizing risks instead of developing innovations. For example, chainsaws come with warning signs telling you not to stop the blade with your bare hands; and take-away coffee mugs come with a warning that the coffee is hot. Sweden is also near the top of the list of countries that behave like over-protective parents. Recently, a Swedish governmental department decided to burn a bus in order to see what happens to buses if they catch fire. However, the experiment was stopped halfway through because the bus 'burned too much'. The public authority as well as the journalists who reported the whole thing complained about how dangerous bus fires were and immediately demanded tougher EU regulations. A brief sentence in the middle of the text reported that the last Swede to die when a bus caught fire was back in 1976.

The problem with living in a world full of over-protective people not willing to take a risk is that you begin to think this is normal behaviour. However, if you step back a bit, you can see how damaging it is to put too much effort into formulating rules and warnings about everything that might go wrong instead of concentrating on things that might turn out well. Rules and safety warnings are all well and good, but they can never replace common sense. One of the main problems of too many rules is that people stop thinking. And if you are not developing yourself there is a risk that you instead spend your energy on creating rules. When Marie Hallander-Larsson became HR Director of the Swedish Post Office, she printed out all the rules and regulations that could be found on the Intranet and which a new employee was expected to read. The pile of paper was 1.7 metres high.

Alan Zhang, Senior Business Developer at the Chinese Internet company Baidu says that there is too much 'rules management' in the West, whereas in China, they use what he calls 'people management'. "We only have two rules: no smoking indoors and no pets allowed in the office. Otherwise you can do what you like." Arthur Duan started off as the HR Manager of the rapidly-growing Sina.com, another successful Chinese Internet company and China's leading Internet portal (similar to Yahoo in the USA). He says that Sina.com's management style is a combination of American management with a Chinese twist. The founders got their education in the USA, so they have an American style of management that they have tailored to suit the Chinese environment. When I asked him to pinpoint the main difference he said, **"Americans aren't used to taking risks."** I asked him to repeat what he had just said in order to make sure I had understood him correctly. Surely he did not mean that the 'venture capitalist country of the world', built up by immigrants who did not know what was waiting for them in the new country, was a country that did not take risks? That is exactly what Arthur Duan meant. According to him, American management is based to an unhealthy extent on having enough background material comprising of surveys, statistics and research before being able to make a decision. Claiming that the Americans are unwilling to take risks is almost like saying that there is no ice in the North Pole, but when Arthur explained what he meant, I suddenly understood.

Chinese management is all about doing – not about planning actions. Arthur explained that managers should encourage employees to establish goals and know where they want to go, but not write long reports about how to get there. This management style is a development of previous leadership in China. It is a more progressive style where the focus is on taking responsibility while also getting things done. It is completely different to the infamous style of Chinese leadership that has resulted in mining accidents or poisoned milk powder scandals where the focus was on short-term attempts to maximize profits. You can still find this kind of irresponsible leadership in China today, but the style that Arthur describes takes the best from the Chinese way (its speed) and combines it with the best from the West (taking responsibility).

As the world around us changes, so too must we change with it. In a fast-changing China, you cannot base all your decisions on research that risks becoming irrelevant. Above all, you cannot waste time on writing reports that detail exactly how to reach your goals. Arthur went on to describe the difference between the Chinese leadership style of today and that of a decade ago. Ten years ago, the Chinese did as they were told without thinking about why. Nowadays, the Chinese ask themselves what they should do and why, and then they just get on and do it. The difference this makes is enormous. Naturally, this change has not taken place in all organizations in a country as large as China, but it is occurring in more and more companies at a rapid pace.

India is also undergoing a similar transformation. I met a representative of the Indian government at an innovation conference in Pune. He shared his views on how people in developed countries see risks and uncertainties compared with those in developing countries. **"We understand the meaning of uncertainty, because in India, everything is uncertain. Nothing is predictable. We are better at living with insecurity and this is part of our comfort zone, if you like. We embrace risk-taking in all its forms: using a new product, testing new technology, trying out new ways of teaching or starting up a new venture. We have gone from being afraid of taking risks to a nation full of gutsy people willing to dare more. And today there are no limitations. In any area, anywhere there are opportunities, you can find people who are willing to seize them."**

Apple is very often cited as being one of the most creative companies in the world, no matter whether you speak to someone living in

Stockholm, Toronto, Seoul or Mumbai. Apple's founder and CEO, Steve Jobs, is considered to be one of the most innovative business people in the world. He is a good example of the curiosity that distinguishes a developing person.

In a speech Jobs gave at Stanford University in 2005, he said this: "Your time is limited, so don't waste it living someone else's life. Don't be trapped by dogma — which is living with the results of other people's thinking. Don't let the noise of others' opinions drown out your own inner voice. And, most importantly, have the courage to follow your heart and intuition. They somehow already know what you truly want to become. Everything else is secondary." He concluded his speech by quoting the parting words of The Whole Earth Catalogue: "Stay Hungry. Stay Foolish." Jobs is passionate about encouraging people to follow their inner voice and to dare take risks in order to achieve their goals.

Apple is a creative, successful and risk-taking Western company. I do not want to portray the developed world as being devoid of people willing to take risks. However, a broader comparison of people's willingness to take risks reveals how unwilling, on the whole, the people in developed countries usually are. You could say that they seem to be too busy protecting what they already have.

There is a fundamental difference between the developed and the developing worlds when it comes to taking risks – and this has its consequences. If you live in a country where you do not know if the electricity is going to work on any given day, then you get used to not taking life for granted. And when your world is always changing at a fast pace, you are forced to be aware and take risks. In an uncertain and unpredictable world, you survive by changing quickly, seizing any opportunities that present themselves, and being flexible enough to take a chance because you do not know what tomorrow will bring.

It is difficult to force yourself to become better at taking risks; to push yourself to step out of your comfort zone. It is more comfortable to live with the illusion of security – but sooner or later you will have to take a risk or two. Perhaps the time to do this is now.

In order to dare take risks and implement your ideas, you have to believe in what you are doing. Perhaps the greatest change that has taken place in the developing world during the past few years is the way people there look at themselves. They now have enough confidence to believe in their own abilities.

Increased self-confidence

Crowded around the main entrance to Hongik University in Seoul, South Korea, is a large cluster of young, fashionable and cheerful Koreans. 50 metres away, a live rock band is playing music on the street. A group carrying TV camera equipment strolls past. An art student is showing her paintings outside a shop; the paintings are beautiful and so is she. A surprisingly large number of Koreans are beautiful. This is not only because they put money and energy into their clothes, hairstyles and plastic surgery. They have that little extra too: an aura of confidence and self-assurance. As you know, a strong belief in yourself makes you attractive. And, believe me, the Koreans believe in themselves. They know that they can compete with anyone. When I asked a Korean industrial designer if she was slightly cowed by the designers in the West, she replied, "I've seen their portfolios and they aren't that good."

You can see this same self-confidence in many developing countries. Like Latvia, for example. Peak Time is the biggest international competition for business students in Europe and is arranged by the Stockholm School of Economics in Riga. During the competition, guest lecturers are invited to speak and I was lucky enough to be chosen a few years ago. After my speech, I spoke to a teacher who said that she thought the students at the School of Economics in Latvia were smarter, more creative and, above all, more motivated than their counterparts in Stockholm. I thought that this was a little strange as we have not seen that many new innovative companies coming out of Latvia. **They still lack confidence in themselves," she said. Then added, "But that is changing."** I spoke to some of the Eastern European students about what they thought of themselves and their possibilities. And sure enough – they spoke with passion and their eyes glowed with enthusiasm. When I asked them why we did not see more innovations coming out of Eastern Europe, I got the same answer time and again, "We had no self-confidence," and then, as if they had been practising it, "but this is changing." The day after my visit to Riga, I had dinner with Aashid Sawjani, who used to work for the Swedish Trade Council in India. He just happened to be on business in Sweden. "It is just wonderful to see the difference that self-confidence has made to young Indians today compared to how they were a few years ago," he burst out as we were chatting about everything from smart energy solutions to the development of innovation in India. This lack of confidence is disappearing as more and more people in developing countries – no matter whether they are East European students, researchers in Africa, Indian professors or publicity managers in Singapore – start to compare what they can do with what is being done in the developed world.

Calvin Soh works in advertising in Singapore. He is Vice-Chairman and Chief Creative Officer at the advertising firm Publicis. Calvin, who comes from Singapore, worked in New York at the advertising agency Fallon when it was considered to be one of the world's most creative firms. As creative director at one of the top American advertising agencies, where he worked with multi-national brands, you could say that he was at the peak of his career. He is now back in Singapore as he was attracted by the challenges and creativity that he saw there – something which he had not seen before. Calvin too puts it down to an increased sense of self-confidence. "You need confidence to be comfortable with the uncomfortable. If – ten or twenty years ago – you had asked an American Edison and a Singaporean one to invent a new lighting system, then the Singaporean Edison would have made a candle with forty wicks. **We just didn't have the confidence to dare try out something new. But all that is changing now."** Calvin explained that this transformation gradually started taking place in the 1990s, but has really taken off during the past few years. Internet access is one of the most important factors for this attitude change. The fact that the same information is now available no matter whether you live in Singapore or New York means that many people in the developing world no longer feel like country hicks, which, of course, contributed to the feeling of low self-esteem. He believes that the younger generation is going to take over the global creative scene because they are better equipped to compete creatively than he ever was. Or as he put it, "When we were a young developing country, we were preoccupied with getting food on the table, with feeding our stomachs. Now we have time to start feeding our minds."

At the same time, as many people in developing countries have gained an increased sense of self-esteem and belief in their own abilities, their respect for the developed world has decreased. Many people I interviewed mentioned that the near-farcical elections in the USA in 2000 had an unexpected effect in developing countries. "If the Americans can't hold a decent election, then maybe they are not as good as we think they are," was a common reaction. The events of 11th September 2001 and the USA's confused reaction to them have also contributed to a lessening respect for developed countries like the US.

And with the win by Barack Obama in the most recent election the effect for people in developing countries has not been so much "I have to go to the US", but more "If that guy who grew up in Indonesia can make it on the world stage - then so can I."

If you tie a horse to a tree time and time again, you eventually only need to place the reins on a tree stump for it to stay put. In much the same way, when developing countries repeatedly heard how advanced the developed world was, then that became an accepted truth: as if there was an unwritten law that certain countries would always be more advanced than others. Nowadays, however, we realize that this is not the truth at all. When I gave a lecture to 250 enthusiastic MBA students in Mumbai, the whole place was just brimming with energy. As I felt their strong faith in themselves, I realized that they seemed to have lost all respect for the West. An interview with a 25-year-old student after my lecture confirmed my suspicions. "I do not feel intimidated by the Western world – or by anybody," she declared. "I'm convinced that our ideas are just as good as yours and that we can challenge anyone with our creativity."

The last two hundred years in China's history, when they have not been considered to be one of the major global economies, is referred to by the Chinese as 'the little dip'. The Chinese know their history, and they know that they have been one of the world's superpowers for much of it. They are convinced that they will soon be a power to be reckoned with again in the near future. "It's our turn now."

Millions of creative people in developing countries are no longer willing to accept that a small part of Western Europe and the USA have the sole right to create and be creative. They are full of confidence – and they are getting impatient.

We are living in exciting times. Developing countries have benefits that we cannot even see. It is a drawback for us that we do not have their advantages. And the fact that we do not even realize that we can learn from these countries is surely our biggest disadvantage.

OUR DISADVANTAG

About what is not happening in the developed world and **the disadvantages of living in a world that defines itself as being developed**, as well as a look at the negative consequences of this.

Dark glasses of **self-righteousness**

While people in developing countries are nearly always refreshingly curious about what is happening in the whole world, a worrying number of people in the developed world are surprisingly indifferent to what is going on in the parts of the world that are not 'their own'. This is true of most areas, including culture. Cecilia Andersson is a Swedish curator who has worked overseas for more than 18 years before returning to Sweden. On her return, she was shocked by how uninterested Swedes were about what was going on in other parts of the world. I met her in Shanghai where she was preparing an exhibition of Chinese artists that she wanted to bring back to Sweden. She is passionate about changing the narrow view of the world that she found back home in her native Sweden.

"It is as if we Swedes are living in our own little bubble. Our lack of interest constantly diminishes us. Here we are in an isolated corner of the world, and we're going to end up without access to a richer life, and without access to a lot of knowledge and creativity. Life is about learning from other cultures in a generous way."

Genco Berk was born in Istanbul, raised in Germany and Turkey and went to the USA for architectural studies. He has worked in Canada, Germany and spent 14 years in Austria. A couple of years ago, he moved to Shanghai. In other words, he is a person who has a lot of experience of living in both the developing and the developed worlds. He has also travelled the world in his job as architect and has done everything from building eco-friendly houses in Japan to designing wine bars in Shanghai. "People in developed countries are living in an illusion created by the media. They are living inside a glass bubble. If you live in a developed culture, you think you are right all the time because that is the information the media feeds you with," he told me. "Maybe this isn't so important if you do not work with creativity. But if you are working in a creative field, you have to be open to all kinds of information because, at the end of the day, you never know where the next creative spark or inspiration is going to come from."

Swedish-born Johan Björksten, who has been living in China for more than 15 years and manages one of China's most successful independent PR firms, agrees with Cecilia Andersson and Genco Berk. He often travels to Sweden to encourage Swedish companies and managers to broaden their horizons. **"The narrow-mindedness of developed countries means that we are limiting our own world view. It means we have fewer sources where we can market our creativity, and it means it is much more difficult for us to understand the Chinese consumers when we compete with Chinese companies on their own market. It also means that we do not understand how to manage our relationship with increasingly strong counterparts in Asia."**

During my interviews for this book, the lack of interest from the rest of the world is a theme that reared its head time and time again. My interviewees have described — with fear and surprise — how Westerners think that the most exciting ideas can only come from their part of the world. One shining example is Hari Kishan Nallan. She is a young industrial designer from India, who got a stipend to study in France. She was astonished that her French classmates were so uninterested in Indian design. She already had a pretty clear picture of what life in France would be like as she had watched French films, followed the news on CNN and the BBC and had met and talked to several French people. When I asked her if coming to a French design college was a culture shock, she replied, "Yes — for my classmates. Most of the French in my class had never met an Indian before and they wondered, for example, why I did not have a red spot on my forehead."

Another example of this kind of attitude is when I gave a lecture at the College of Arts, Crafts and Design in Stockholm for industrial design undergraduates. I told the audience what Hari Kishan Nallan had said about the lack of knowledge about other parts of the world. After my lecture, a Brazilian exchange student came up to me and told me with a sigh that it was not only in France that students did not know — or did not want to know — about design from other countries. After six months in Sweden, she had not been asked a single question about Brazilian design by her classmates. "If the opposite happened and a Swede came to my college, then we would have overwhelmed her with questions on her very first day," she declared.

Joachim Rosenberg, manager of Volvo Trucks in Asia is worried about our lack of interest in developing countries. A strategy based on not knowing so much about 'them' is all very well when the markets for most products are to be found in Europe and the USA. But as India and China are now two of the largest and most important markets for nearly all products, this approach is no longer viable. "We don't want them to enter our half of the playing field, but if we don't go into their half, then we can never win the match. It isn't just about lack of knowledge: it's a kind of ignorance. **Our dark glasses of self-righteousness prevent us from seeing what is really happening."** Of course, neither my interviewees nor I mean that people in developed countries are completely uneducated about the world. We do, however, have less knowledge than many others. By defining general knowledge as mainly knowing things about the Western world, we have unconsciously walled in our curiosity. It is time to get a grasp of the whole picture: in other words, to become someone who knows about the most important events going on in the world today.

By limiting our field of knowledge to those things that come mainly from our own developed part of the world, we are also limiting our ability to be creative. Especially as more and more innovations are now being created in the developing world; innovations that we do not even see.

Both eyes open

A new idea arises when you combine at least two known ideas in a new way. **One of the greatest advantages that the people in developing countries have compared to those in developed countries is the fact that they know about 'our' part of the world as well as theirs.** This leads to a greater understanding of what is going on in the whole of the world, which means that they have access to more ideas that they can combine in new ways.Due to more open attitudes to the West and the globalization of Western brands, people in developing countries are exposed to large parts of Western culture and lifestyles – like Amanda, for example. Amanda is a 29-year-old Chinese, whom I got to know when I lived in Beijing. She had never been abroad when I first met her, and had spent her entire life in China. However, this did not mean that she lived a narrow life with no clue as to what was happening outside the borders of the Middle Kingdom. Quite the opposite. Amanda enjoys drinking coffee at an American Starbucks while listening to the Swedish singer, Robyn, on her American iPod. Her favourite TV series is the American Sex and the City (watched on pirated DVDs). When she can afford a car, she wants to buy a German BMW. Amanda is, of course, also being exposed to Chinese and Asian cultures and the local products, services and customs that are connected to these cultures. A Chinese person who has never been abroad – someone like Amanda – knows about Nike and Li-Ning, Tiger Woods and Yao Ming, Madonna and Rain. A Sri Lankan watches both Bollywood and Hollywood movies; and if you go to the cinema in Singapore, you can see films in Chinese, English, Hindi and Malay. Locally produced films in Singapore often have dialogue in two or more languages in the same film.

In South Korea, teams of breakdancers known as B-Boys are popular. Korean teams like Gambler are among the best in the world and take part in competitions in the USA and Europe. Until recently, leading B-boy competitions in the West were not even open to teams from other parts of the world. When they were finally allowed to compete, Gambler won the first Western competition they entered. Their success has kick started a wave of breakdancing in South Korea and there are now thousands of teams. Gambler has signed a sponsor agreement worth hundreds of thousands of dollars and has toured Vietnam, Hong Kong and Mongolia with great success.

Hip hop and luxury items. Film stars and sports trends. People in developing countries keep an eye on what is going on in their part of the world – and in ours. How much does a European or American know about Asia, for example? How many Asian trendsetters can they name? How many designers, leaders or entrepreneurs do they know? How many artists, writers or company managers are they familiar with? And can they even name the leaders of China and India? Can they give me the name of just one living Bollywood star? Usually they can not.

Now, of course, not everyone who lives in a developing country knows everything about what is happening in their world and our own. And not everyone in developed countries is completely clueless about what is going on in the developing world. **"Things aren't as bad as you paint them!" protest people at the lectures I give in Sweden.** What they mean is that they do have essential knowledge about other countries. Either that – or they mean that it is not fair to compare a Westerner with little education and well-travelled people in developing countries.

Unfortunately, they are wrong.

In September 2007 Sweden's most comprehensive contemporary encyclopaedia, invited me to hold a lecture at the Knowledge Awards 2007 that they had arranged in order to raise awareness about the value of knowledge. The cream of Sweden's 'knowledge elite' was present. And as the organizers had asked me to give 'a provocative and eye-opening' lecture, I grabbed the chance to test the level of knowledge of the audience. I asked them who the leader of China and India were. If they knew the names of ten Chinese companies with potential global brands. I showed them a picture of Yao Ming, the basketball star, and asked how many of them knew what he was called. The results were depressing. Less than 1% of the audience, chosen to represent how knowledgeable Swedes are, could answer my questions. I think the result would have been similar if I had asked other questions too.

I have asked well-educated Swedes all kinds of questions about developing countries and the results are always just as disappointing. In general terms, we know very little. For example, I have asked groups of people to name ten living people in developing countries that will affect the development of the world in some area, be it within culture, politics, sport, business or education. Less than 1% can actually do this.

When I pose the same question in developing countries and ask the audience to give me the names of ten people in the developed world that will affect the development of the world, a large majority always raise their hands. It is difficult to hear that we know less about the world than those in developing countries and many people choose to give excuses rather than look at the cold facts. Hiding our heads in the sand might feel good, but it will not solve anything. People in the developing world are curious about the world they live in whereas many people in the West live in a bubble where they are largely only exposed to Western culture. It is much easier for a Chinese or an Indian to get access to Western culture than it is for us to access Asian culture. One reason is that so many Western companies are global and have expanded quickly on markets in developing countries. For example, Adidas is planning to open 40 new Adidas stores per month in China – 40 months in a row. That adds up to 1,600 new stores in China in less than three and a half years.

Explaining why a person in a developing country is more exposed to thoughts, ideas, products, services and brands than someone in the developed world is not the most important thing. What is most important is that we reflect on what this might mean. The end result is that 'they' – people from developing countries – are more widely exposed to everything from new ideas and thoughts to products and trends than 'we' – people from developed countries – are. **A greater exposure to all sorts of thoughts, cultures and experiences creates a good breeding-ground for the explosion of new ideas and innovations. They have both their eyes open, whereas we only view the world with one.**

A brilliant example of how knowledge about both the East and the West can lead to new ideas are the Olympic medals that were designed by a Chinese for the Beijing Olympics 2008. As is traditional, the medals were gold for the winner, silver for the runner-up and bronze for third place. However, in China, jade is traditionally used to make jewellery. So, the medals were made of gold and white jade for the winner, silver and yellow jade for the runner-up, and bronze and green jade for third place. How many Western designers would have come up with this idea? How many even know that there is such a thing as yellow jade?

Another simple but clear example of the Chinese ability to take different ideas from around the world and then combine them to produce something new is the Chinese electrical outlet or wall socket. European, American and Asian plugs can all fit into an ordinary Chinese wall socket. This means that very often you do not need an adaptor in China as, generally, electrical devices work no matter where they have been bought. For someone like me, who has travelled around Europe swearing because the plug to my laptop will not fit into the wall sockets, this is a shining example of the Chinese ability to combine old ideas in new ways and improve an existing product. Another example is the buildings in China. The first building I lived in when I moved to China was situated in Jian Wai Soho. The building was of a modern, Scandinavian-style design with lots of light material and huge windows. My apartment was on the eighteenth floor. Actually, to be honest, it was really on the fifteenth floor. The building, just like many others in China, did not have a fourth floor, as the number four is unlucky in Chinese culture, nor did it have a thirteenth floor, as this is considered unlucky in Western culture. Most well educated Chinese know this, but the same cannot be said of most well-educated Westerners.

Yes – my examples are banal; yet they show how someone in a developing country gets in more ideas from different cultures than someone in the West. This gives them more possibilities of combining a broader range of ideas to create new ones. In other words, it is a good breeding-ground for a creative melting pot. Knowledge about the East and the West helped create the universal wall socket, culturally-neutral buildings that are not unlucky and globally-acclaimed Olympic medals. It is this kind of broad knowledge base that gives entrepreneurs in developing countries a head start when it comes to developing global products and services.

Reflect about who has the greatest chance of writing a global bestseller: an author who has grown up with experiences gained from one part of the world, or the one who has grown up with influences from many cultures and who can refer to both Eastern and Western cultures? Which entrepreneur stands the bigger chance of developing a product that is a global success: the one with knowledge about half the world, or the one who knows about the whole world? Who can best understand the political development going on in the world: the person who is curious about the world or the one who thinks that one part of the world is more important than the other? I have met many industrial designers from different parts of the globe. One I met in Delhi had studied in India and Europe. **"I know that a Frenchman has wine in his fridge, but he doesn't know what I keep in mine,"** she told me. **"This means that I can design fridges for the French, but they can't design one for me."** In Istanbul, I met a young Turkish industrial designer who had studied in France. He said something distressingly similar when discussing the disadvantages of his fellow French students. "If you are born in a blue room and grow up in a blue room, then you cannot design a red chair. The French just want to live in their blue room. I need to go out and see all the colours!"

If the 20th century was all about Western companies going global, then the 21st century is about the fast-growing companies from developing countries muscling in on the action and becoming global players too – regardless of whether we are talking about Mittal Steel, the Tata Group or Lenovo. The electronic manufacturer Aigo will compete with Sony and Samsung, and the telecom solutions provider Huawei will be one of Ericsson's contenders. Fashion trends will be created in Shanghai or Mumbai as well as in Paris. In a truly global world, those who are familiar with the whole world will be off to a good start. And right now, it is those living in developing countries that have this head start.

Do you live in a blue room or can you see all of the colours? How much inspiration do you get from the thoughts, ideas, trends, discoveries and innovations that are being created in the developing world at the moment? And what kind of inspiration can you give to others? Where do you find your information? How active are you in getting news from around the world? Blaming the media for not reporting what is going on in other parts of the world is no excuse. We all have access to the Internet and to English language news sites from around the world. The information is there. **What kind of ideas could you come up with if you had more sources of information, inspiration and ideas than you have today?** Perhaps it is time to awaken our curiosity. To show more interest in the rest of the world. To open both our eyes.

Don't follow the recipe

Subiakto Priosoedarsano's name means 'great leader' – and if you have such a name, then it is not so strange perhaps to become the CEO of your own advertising firm. Hotline Advertising is the largest independent advertising company in Jakarta, Indonesia. Subiakto sits in a gigantic office that overlooks the sea of creative people working on the floor below. He enjoys talking in metaphors and uses a long one when describing the difference between people in developing and developed countries. "The way I see it, people in the developed world are stuck in a how things should be done. It's a bit like eating at a good restaurant: you go to the restaurant, look at the menu and then place your order. And that's that.However, living in a developing country is more like going to a food stall on the streets of Asia, where there are no menus. You can choose what you want to eat, and decide for yourself how much of each ingredient should go into your food. If you ask the cook what the dish is called, you'll probably find that it doesn't exist in any cook book. It's a unique dish cooked according to your wishes."

Subiakto went on to say, "You are too stuck in your menus, as it were. That means that it is difficult for you to change as you are so boxed in. You know what to do, but as soon as you know how to do something, this creates fear: the fear of making a mistake. When you follow a given recipe and do something that isn't written down in that recipe, there is the risk that you think you have made a mistake. We, on the other hand, dare to experiment because when you don't follow a recipe, then you can't make a mistake. The big advantage for people like me who don't have a recipe is, of course, that I am right no matter what I cook. It is only after trying out a combination that we find out what it tastes like. If it doesn't taste good, then we improve the combination next time round. And if it tastes good, then we have invented a new dish."

Subiakto has hit the nail on the head when describing the disadvantage of being developed: the belief that everything has been done, convincing ourselves that we have already found the best way of how to do something.

It is when I am in places like Jakarta that I realize how false this way of thinking really is. I asked Subiakto to give his advice to those who feel as if they are always ordering from a menu. Without hesitating, he said: **"Forget all the rules! Get out there and do something creative!"** When we have a long menu to choose from, it is easy to convince ourselves that we are making a free choice. But how free is our choice? How stuck are you in your thought patterns when it comes to doing something? A few years ago, I had the honour of giving a lecture to all the chefs who had won the Chef of the Year competition in Sweden. During the wonderful dinner afterwards, I asked Sweden's best chefs what the connection is between creativity and being a top chef. They were all unanimous in saying that really good chefs never use a recipe but experiment until they come up with something new. They were very surprised about how many people do not dare improvise when cooking. One of the chefs put it like this, "I only follow a recipe when baking bread. How is it possible to create something new if you never break out of those pre-conceived and written down rules that are recipes?"

Even more importantly, perhaps, is to remember that we must dare dream of new things. Unfortunately, this is something that we also seem to have forgotten how to do.

A life without dreams is a nightmare

In the early 1960s, John F. Kennedy had the vision of landing a man on the moon and bringing him home safely within the decade. This vision became a reality in 1969. A whole nation applauded what must be one of the most daring dreams in the history of the world. Magnificent dreams can help people achieve magnificent things. And when a dream is fulfilled, you have to set up new goals. The developed world achieved many of its dreams, but forgot to have new ones – and in this way, it stopped dreaming to a large extent.

In a recently published survey people in Europe were asked this question: "Do you think that the younger generation will have an easier life than your generation?" Less than 10% said yes in Sweden and in Germany only 5% answered positively. In Latvia and Lithuania, however, roughly 50% of those asked said that their children would lead an easier life. The difference here between developed and developing countries is very clear indeed. Ask a Swede if they think that Sweden will be a better country tomorrow than it is today and less than 30% will say yes. Once, when I put this question to a class of high school students only 10% put up their hands. A country in which only a tenth of its young believe that their country will improve in the future is a country without dreams. The results I get in developing countries are totally different. In India, for example, everyone put up their hands when I asked the same question – as they did in South Korea. In Sri Lanka, nearly everyone raised their hands while in China they put up both hands, stood up and started clapping.

I am well aware that this is not a statistically sound survey, but I can tell you this: I have asked this question more than twenty times in developed countries and have never had more than 30% of the audience raise a hand while in developing countries I have never seen less than 80% put up a hand. The difference in attitude when it comes to the future is striking. **People have dreams, but they are not happening in the developed world.** When an overwhelming majority of the population no longer have much hope for the future, then there is an even greater need for new dreams. If you do not have dreams, then they can never come true.

The USA is no longer synonymous with the American Dream – but rather with American Fear these days. Fear of the world, terrorism, losing what they already have. Europe too has stopped dreaming. Well, at least the old Europe has. There is no shortage of dreams or visions in new Europe or the old Soviet states. Perhaps we have stopped dreaming because we are too focused on losing what we have. However, we cannot preserve anything by just looking back. If hope is the last thing to leave people, then where does the Western world stand when a clear majority of its people have no hope of the future getting any better?

The historian Peter Englund said, "Without longing, we are lost." How much longing can exist in a country where 70% of the population does not believe that tomorrow will be better than today? What happens to a country when it stops hoping, longing and dreaming?

Right now, developing countries are the ones with more and bigger dreams. You can get a clear picture of where the biggest dreams are being dreamed by looking at where the tallest buildings in the world are being built. When the USA became the country where hopes flourish, it built the tallest buildings in the world in the form of the Empire State Building and the Sears Tower. The most recent years the tallest buildings in the world have been built in developing countries, such as Malaysia (Twin Towers), Taiwan (Taipei 101), China (Shanghai Financial Centre) and Dubai (Burj Dubai).

Burj Dubai, the world's tallest building, is about 800 metres tall (including the spire), has cost more than $20 billion and is a monument to the sweeping visions, and sometimes daring dreams of Dubai. In Dubai, you can hear talk not only of the tallest building in the world, but also of the world's largest amusement park, grandest shopping centre and biggest airport as well as of the creation of artificial islands. And these are just some of the big dreams that are being made reality here.

It is easy to laugh at the construction of the tallest buildings in the world and to dismiss these ideas as macho projects for countries with a lot of money and too little imagination. Big dreams can result in illusions of grandeur and bad judgement, which can then lead to worse results than just a couple of buildings to brag about. But surely the worst thing of all is to have no dreams at all?

The Eiffel Tower is the global icon of Paris and France these days: a symbol that has lasted over a hundred years. When it was built for the International Exhibition in Paris in 1889, it was a project full of vision and pride. At that time, France wanted to market itself as a country with sweeping dreams and the Eiffel Tower has affected the way each and every French person views Paris. In the same way, the edifices now being constructed in the same spirit of grandeur will serve to remind those living in developing countries of the value of daring to dream.

Other dreams taking place in developing countries are not quite as easy to see. One dark, rainy evening, I took a taxi to the large university complex in northeast Beijing and looked for a lecture hall tucked away on the second floor in order to listen to the South African Mark Shuttleworth. A Beijing friend of mine told me to get there early. In fact, I thought he was kidding when he advised me to get there two hours before the start of the lecture if I wanted to get a seat. When I arrived early, the hall was already filling up but, luckily, I managed to get a seat. When Mark finally turned up on stage, the room was bursting with young Chinese who had come to get a glimpse of him. Mark Shuttleworth is a South African who became a billionaire in the dot-com era by starting an Internet consulting business offering encrypted e-commerce services on the web. He also paid about $20 million to go into space as a 'space tourist' on a Russian spaceflight, thus becoming the first African in space. His latest project is Ubuntu, a free community developed, Linux-based operating system that is so easy to use it can compete with Windows and Mac. Mark travels the world persuading governments and businesses to invest in Ubuntu instead of paying for expensive Apple or Windows licences. He has a dream of making computers accessible to the hundreds of millions of people around the world that cannot even afford to buy a computer.

Of all the people I have met, Mark is probably the one who best personifies a developing person from the developing world. He has many splendid dreams that he makes a reality. During the lecture, several hundred Chinese students stood or sat, totally engrossed in what he had to say. **You could almost hear them thinking, "If he can, then so can I!"** All those big dreams about creating the next new Linux, Apple or even Ubuntu got a real lift that evening. Dreams create the possibility of creating something better than that we already have. They challenge the status quo and give us a glimpse of how things could be.

There is a saying that goes: "Good is the enemy of great." In other words, by saying that something is 'good enough' we miss the opportunity of turning it into something so much better. **We could even extend the saying so that it goes: "Great is the enemy of dreams coming true."** By defining a society (or a company, organization or individual) as being developed, by believing that we already have a solution that is great, we miss the potential that can be found in having daring new dreams. If you do not have new dreams, then they cannot come true – and we also miss the chance to improve on things that already exist.

An experience on a Bangkok street clearly conveyed this feeling of how we, in the developed world, have missed out on a better world by not dreaming anymore. Thailand is a country of illusions and if you are only there for a few days, it is easy to think that it is just about cheap beer, cheap massages and cheap tourism. But behind the easy smiles there hides another Thailand: one that has decided to preserve its culture – and sell it to tourists – while also continuing to develop.

One day as I was wandering around aimlessly on the streets of Bangkok, trying to get a grip on this vibrant city, I walked past a shining white building. It had a large display window through which I could make out a beautiful-looking reception area. The design was so stunning that I assumed this was a newly-opened design hotel so I decided to go in and see if they had any rooms available. They did not because it turned out that this was not a hotel – but a dentist! In fact, it called itself a dental spa. I was so stunned that I decided to go to the dentist during my holiday. The place was just amazing. The dentistry was equipped with the latest dental equipment and a flat screen TV on the wall played a James Bond film while I waited for the anaesthetic to take effect. The tray that the dental assistant brought in had small flowers on it and the only difference to that of a spa was that it had a toothbrush on it instead of a cup of tea. It felt as if I were partly at the dentist's and partly at a spa.

"Can this really be a dental surgery?" I thought to myself.

On my return to Sweden, it struck me that going to the dentist at home had not really changed for the better in over twenty years. When I was growing up in Sweden in the 1970s, I was always hearing that we had 'the best dental care in the world' and 'the best healthcare and welfare in the world'. We all believed this, and it was probably true.

What has happened since then in both Sweden and Europe? Did we stop dreaming about how to improve dental and health care because we already thought it was the best? In countries where 70% of the population does not think that life will be better in the future, then there is a sad lack of hope and dreams.

As people, we do not seem to know where we are headed nor what we are expected to take part in and create. We realize that we must do something, but we do not know what, how or why. The results are confusion and resignation. In part, this is because our politicians lack visions and dreams and this attitude then trickles down to the rest of society. However, it is too simplistic just to blame it all on politicians as it can never be solely another person's responsibility to see that we keep on dreaming and that we make these dreams a reality.

How big are your own dreams? What hopes do you hold for the future when it comes to your own country? If we do not believe that tomorrow will get better, then the future will never improve. The Western world may view dreams as being unnecessary, but they are perhaps just what we need right now.

But it is not only the lack of dreams and hope that limit the people of the developed world. Our tendency to impose artificial boundaries on ourselves is just as limiting.

Artificial **boundaries**

Chuck Trent is the CIO (Chief Information Officer) at the telecoms giant Cisco Asia/Pacific. Asia has quickly become one of the most important markets for Cisco. I met Chuck at a seminar in Sri Lanka where we were both guest lecturers at a conference about the future. Even though he has worked in the IT business for 36 years, he said that it has never been as much fun as it has been for the past three or four years since he started working in developing countries in Asia. Yes – he thought the PC revolution was big and the dot-com era exciting; but they are nothing compared to what is going on in the developing world at the moment. The energy and endless possibilities are so much greater these days.

A few years ago, Cisco had 400 employees in India working with software development. Today they have 4000 employees. The company intends to invest more than a billion dollars in Cisco India as well as starting a venture capital fund of 100 million dollars to invest in Indian companies. In addition, they are planning to invest 16 billion dollars in China. In spite of these huge sums, Cisco is not after cheap production. **"It's not about low cost," declared Chuck "It's about the availability of talent – and the ability to be innovative."**

Less than five minutes into our conversation and Chuck had already named 'innovation' as being an argument for employing people from developing countries. When I interrupted him to say that many people in the West will think that I am misquoting him by reporting that he thinks creativity is greater in India and China than it is in the West, he laughed knowingly. "What we found was that when we put a business problem to our employees in the USA, they would often come up with fifteen reasons as to why there was no good solution. But in Asia, and especially in Bangalore, employees would rush to the whiteboard and ask, 'What would it take to fix the problem? What do we have to do and what kind of skills do we need to find a solution?' Developing countries do not have the classic reaction that there is only one way of doing something."

Chuck's employees at Cisco in India ask, "What can we do?" and "How can we come up with a new solution?" In the USA, he thinks that people are more likely to say that nothing can be done. So, according to Cisco, an American company in one of the most innovative lines of business you can find, the people in developing countries are more open to finding solutions while people in developed countries make excuses not to find them. Time and time again, people confirm my suspicions that those in the developing world are more creative because they are not stuck in a narrow thinking pattern when it comes to what is possible.

You probably know about the classic psychological experiment where two groups are set the task of building a bridge out of logs over a stream. The first group is shown a bridge that has already been built. The second group is given no clue – only a pile of logs. Before the groups start building their bridges, the researchers secretly make the stream wider so that it is no longer possible to build a bridge in the same way as was shown to the first group. The first group then went on to try and build a bridge that was similar to the one they had seen. The second group had no pre-conceptions about what the bridge 'should' look like, so they looked for a solution that would suit the circumstances. It was easier for the second group to find a solution than it was for the first one. What this experiment shows is that having knowledge about how something 'should' be solved can be limiting at times as it stops us from seeing the new answers that might have evolved along with the changing world. In other words, people from developing countries have the advantage of not being as trapped in set thought patterns about how things must be done.

Chuck believes that not only have people in developing countries become more innovative, but that those in developed countries have also lost a bit of their creative edge by becoming less hungry and less open to change. **"The most important thing for us to realize is that making up at least seventeen excuses as to why a problem cannot be solved is a very ineffective way of working. We have to learn a new way of looking at issues and just flip things around. This is what they have done in the developing world. They have learnt to take business problems and then flip them upside down and start**

looking for possibilities instead. And this is what we can really learn from them: how to turn a challenge into an opportunity."

After a moment's reflection, Chuck added, "They don't have the artificial boundaries that we have created in other parts of the world. These boundaries are not real, though. They are our own creations – and they are ours to break down."

Are you stuck when it comes to how things should be done? How could you turn the most common reasons for not doing something into an opportunity to find new ways and solutions? Which artificial boundaries are limiting you? And what can you do to break out of these boundaries and find new possibilities?

Just because life is good does not mean it cannot get any better. Being ahead does not mean that we should not try even harder to develop ourselves. Being number one is, in fact, an extremely dangerous position to be in.

We are number one – so **why try harder?**

Ericsson is often called the flagship of Sweden. During the past hundred years or so, it has succeeded in going from small local company to becoming a global leader in the telecommunications industry, one of the hottest and largest growing businesses in recent years. Ericsson was one of the most valuable companies on the Stockholm stock exchange and one of the largest private employers in Sweden. At one time, it had more than 60,000 employees in Sweden and over 100,000 around the world. It looked unsinkable – but then something happened. Ericsson is still a market leader today, but the number of employees has been more than halved in Sweden. The telecoms business is perhaps the business that most clearly reflects the rapid changes that are occurring. In just over a decade, countries like India, China and Indonesia have gone from being small areas with potential to becoming some of the most important markets with the strongest growth. Add to this the parallel development between the Internet and telecommunications that has resulted in the convergence of data and telephony, two of the fastest growing businesses, and you get a new business called communications. You could say that Ericsson is in the middle of two major changes at the same time. So, how has the company succeeded in adapting itself to meet the new rules?

An employee working at Ericsson's global education department summed it up like this: "Reaction time is very slow." In other words, a large, established company that has been a market leader for a long time has now found itself in a situation where it has become very hard for the organization to see the important changes that are occurring right under its nose. Having many years of experience can be a comfort factor in much the same way that a large tanker floats with more stability than a small boat. Yet, it takes that tanker much longer to make a turn. In the same way, systems create a sluggishness that makes organizations slow, and this, in turn, increases the risk that they will not be able to make the turn in time.

Ericsson is a classic example of a developed organization: a market leader that has not fully seen, understood or adapted itself to the new circumstances it finds itself in – which is why it runs the risk of being shipwrecked.

Developed companies with long years behind them as leaders in their businesses are at risk of being hit hard when challenged by upstarts in the form of developing companies. Petter Andersson, LM Ericsson's Education Manager, explained the difficulties they have had internally of creating an awareness of future challenges. "As a global leader, you always run the risk of looking at things too narrow-mindedly. It can be hard to motivate staff to beat the competitors when you have already done that so many times before." This is a classic example of the 'I am number one – so why try harder?' syndrome. Ericsson really has succeeded in beating its competitors year after year when it comes to mobile applications just as Nokia has dominated the mobile cell phone market. But as Petter said soberly, "You can't build future victories based on old wins." Ericsson now has a new competitor in the form of Huawei, a developing company from China. If you imagined that the two companies were boxers getting ready to fight it out, you might say this:"Here is the current champion Ericsson with a history that is more than a century old, weighing in with many experienced workers, long-term customer relations and a market share of 29%. And here, in the other corner, we have the newcomer Huawei that has only been around for twenty years, weighing in with an average age of under 30 and a global market share of 8% within the area of mobile infrastructure." On paper, Huawei may not look much of a threat to a giant like Ericsson, but as the boxer Mike Tyson can bitterly attest, being the current champion is no guarantee that you will automatically continue winning. And just like Tyson, many developed companies risk a painful and late awakening if they do not realize what is happening.

It seems as if realization has dawned on Ericsson's previous CEO, Carl-Henrik Svanberg – at least, according to the Japanese entrepreneur Sachio Senmoto whom I met in Kyoto at one of my lectures.

"Fredrik San," he said. "Let me tell you a story." Sachio had been in Stockholm visiting the Ericsson headquarters. As he was an important customer, the company decided that he should dine with Carl-Henrik Svanberg. According to Sachio, "I got him drunk and took the opportunity to ask him what he was most afraid of. 'Huawei,' he answered."

Carl-Henrik had, quite simply, realized that Huawei is a developing company in a business where Ericsson is developed. The company is known in China as one where the employees work extremely hard to reach their goals. Huawei may be a young company, but it was not born yesterday. It has 70% of the world's 50 largest mobile operators as customers. And it overtook Ericsson in the number of patent submissions it has. Huawei is now fourth on the list of global patent submissions.

When I asked some managers at China Mobile, one of the world's largest mobile operators, which company (Ericsson or Huawei) was more innovative, they replied, **"Ericsson is an old man, experienced and a little dull. Huawei is a young man, enthusiastic and much more creative."** According to these managers, Huawei is a threat not because they are cheaper but because they are more innovative. When I was at a workshop on creativity that was sponsored by Ericsson no less, I asked some of the managers from China Telecom, China's largest state-owned telecom operator, which were the most innovative companies in the world. They said, "Apple, Google and Huawei." After my lecture at the R&D department of Ericsson in China, a young Chinese came up to me and whispered, "When we work really fast and creatively here at Ericsson in China, then people usually say that we are working the 'Huawei way'."

Even when the management of a developed company realizes that their new competitor is a developing company and that it is time to take the threat seriously, it can still be difficult – nearly impossible, in fact – to get the rest of the organization on board and start changing the way they do things.

Another clear example of developed companies being challenged by a developing one is the airline business in Europe when it faced a new player on the scene: Ryanair. When Ryanair started offering flights for just a fraction of the price offered by the established market leaders in the airline business in European countries, many of the competitors laughed out loud. People thought it was obvious that no passenger would ever agree to pay extra for their luggage, not get any food on the flight and then land at an airport outside the main city. No one thought that Ryanair presented much of a challenge. However, in recent years, Ryanair has become one of the most profitable airline companies in Europe. Several former SAS employees have told me that SAS never really succeeded in realizing that a low-price company like Ryanair would actually shake up the airline business. The most worrying thing of all, however, is that even though they have acknowledged the threat of low-cost airlines, they still have not succeeded in making the necessary changes. They have reduced the price of their tickets without changing the way they do business, which is, to a large extent, still based on a time when they could sell expensive fares. They had to sell their assets to stay afloat in the middle of an economic boom. According to one of the managers at an SAS affiliate who has been on the management board for more than ten years, SAS has found it difficult to adapt to the new competition. They have reduced their prices but not their costs. This is not, of course, a viable long-term strategy. All developing companies have to make sure that they themselves do not fall into the same trap of no longer seeing new solutions. After many years of pushing the boundaries of the airline business, it seems as if Ryanair has lost some of its pioneering spirit during recent years.

If you want to study the most interesting example of a young and hungry developing company in the airline business, then you should look towards Malaysia. In October 2001, AirAsia stood on the brink of bankruptcy and was bought up by businessman Tony Fernandes for 25 cents. In just eight years it has become one of Asia's most exciting companies, managing to combine the business methods of the low-price companies and the image and branding of the high-price ones. While Ryanair has the reputation of being 'cheap but shoddy', AirAsia has the image of being 'cool and cheap'. The airline sponsors the football club Manchester United and a Formula 1 team and the in-flight staff wear baseball caps instead of the more traditional old-fashioned ones. The company has flights to all the countries in ASEAN as well as flying to Australia and Europe from its main airport in Kuala Lumpur. The inter-Asian flights often cost just a handful of Euros. In 2008, the magazine Fast Company nominated AirAsia as one of the world's 50 most innovative companies. It was the only Asian brand to receive the honour and the only airline too.

Developing companies do not have to come from developing countries: Ryanair comes from Ireland, after all. But the chances are much greater these days that many developing companies will not come from the developed world.

Let's take a look at the 'Ryanair' of the car industry in the form of a company from India. At the start of 2008, the Indian car manufacturer Tata Motors presented their new car, the Tata Nano, at a car fair in Delhi. By pretending to be a Swedish journalist, I managed to sneak into the private press conference where the Tata Nano was presented for the very first time. Together with what must have been a thousand journalists and car experts from around the world, I waited expectantly. When the car was finally unveiled, total chaos ensued as everyone wanted to see it as close up as possible. The Tata Nano is a completely new kind of car. It can carry four passengers and retails for 100,000 Indian rupees, which is about $2,000. The launch of this car has halved the price you can now pay for the world's cheapest car. Tata Motors has shown the lazy and tired developed companies that it is possible to produce a method of transportation at a much lower price than the automobile business thought possible.

At the press conference, I asked a Japanese journalist what he thought was going through the minds of a Japanese company like Honda today. "In tomorrow's article, I 'm going to write that they should be very, very afraid." When I recounted this remark at a lecture I gave in Sweden, a man put up his hand and introduced himself as a manager for one of Sweden's major car brands. "We are also very scared," he said. If Tata Motors can make a great little car like the Tata Nano for $2,000, then just think how much greater a car they will be able to produce for $20,000. When companies from low-cost countries, used to competing by being the cheapest, start to combine their low-cost mentality with creativity and innovation, the result is the equivalent of the leopard of the business world: a small, quick player with the potential to be frighteningly effective.

The developing company Huawei is challenging Ericsson, the Tata Nano is threatening the car industry and the airline business has met its match in Ryanair and AirAsia. Certain lines of business are only just realizing that unexpectedly dangerous upstarts are challenging them. For example, ABB has now understood that Huaming, which only a few years ago was a harmless low-cost company, nowadays can offer a much broader range in certain areas than ABB can. However, most businesses have not yet really been challenged by a developing company – or, if they have, then they do not understand what their former non-threatening competitor can now do.

If you want to cure yourself, you must first realize that you are sick. If you want to appreciate the extent to which a developed country imprisons you, you must first absorb and understand the disadvantages of living in a part of the world that sees itself as complete. But not all is lost: when I moved to China four years ago, it was because – from my narrow point of view – I thought the most interesting story would be what we in the West could teach them. I soon realized, however, that what they could teach us was far more remarkable.

WHAT CAN WE LEARN FROM THEM?

About what we in the developed world can
learn from people in developing countries.

Copy Tigers – very large and strong Copy Cats

The ability to emulate a master is regarded as a good thing in many Asian cultures. Trying to imitate a master is a form of appreciation and respect. By copying, you are in effect saying, "Master! You have managed to do something in the best way possible, and by copying you, I hope to become a master myself one day." In the West, we call this kind of behaviour copying and think that it is something ugly. In fact, we view the willingness of Chinese companies to copy as something negative, as a reason why China will never be able to compete when it comes to innovation. Many Westerners laugh or swear at the Chinese when they see them taking photos of everything at a fair or exhibition. "All the Chinese do is copy," they moan – as if you cannot be creative if you take a look at what others are doing.

When I was in Beijing, I once sat on a panel with representatives from Sony Ericsson, Nokia and Motorola. The moderator asked us for our views on China and copying, and all the representatives from the major mobile manufacturers said more or less the same thing: that China could never be innovative if they did not stop copying. At last, it was my turn. I looked at the three representatives of the largest phone companies in the world and said, "So – which one of you invented the mobile phone? Because that means that the other two must have copied you." My point was that all companies copy to some extent or other. The notion that people in the East can only copy while those in the West come up with original ideas and do not copy is nonsense. **In fact, you have to copy to be creative.** By combining brush with tooth, we came up with the toothbrush; laser and LP records became CDs. Edison took his newly-discovered bulb and paired it with the idea of the neck of a bottle in order to invent an easy way of screwing a light bulb into place. Einstein's equation $E = mc2$ took for granted that someone else had already defined E, =, m, c and squared. When Sir Isaac Newton described how he discovered the laws of gravity, he said he did it by 'standing on the shoulders of giants'. He would never have discovered these laws if he had not used and developed thoughts and ideas that already existed. All ideas arise when someone, consciously or unconsciously, combines at least two known things. In other words, all creativity is, to some extent, a form of copying.

Many people make the mistake of confusing copying with illegal copying when they criticize companies that copy. Pirated copies of goods are wrong – and illegal. Infringing the intellectual copyright of other companies is also wrong – and just as illegal. China has shown a great lack of respect for the intellectual copyright of others, but increased efforts to put a stop to the illegal copying of goods in China has started to show results. It is now harder to find pirated products than it was five years ago. However, it should be remembered that not all copying is illegal – or even wrong. Imitating a master can often by useful, effective and good. What Western companies do not seem to realize when they complain about the Chinese learning from their competitors is that they should be doing the same. Many Westerners do not believe that they have anything to learn from others while companies in developing countries are some of the best in the world when it comes to realizing that they do not know everything. And that is why they travel the world examining what others are doing. **The ability to be inspired by others and copy good solutions is not the opposite of creativity – but an indispensable part of it.**

Google is often cited as being the most innovative organization in the world. But what did they invent? They did not invent search engines; they copied them from AltaVista. They did not come up with AdWords; they copied this from Overture. They did not come up with the idea of Google Earth; a company they bought did. Google has not invented its best ideas but copied and improved on the innovations of others. Apple copied its graphical user interface from Xerox, and they even copied the concept of the computer mouse. Steve Jobs did not invent anything new; rather Apple saw the value of other people's innovations and then copied and implemented them into their own business. You see, innovation is all about being able to copy in an effective and original way.

Developing companies are the ones that understand the importance and value of copying things in the right way. Developed companies, on the other hand, think that they are the only ones who are innovative and that is why they refuse to be inspired by the ideas of others. When a Chinese manufacturer makes an exact copy of an iPod, it winds up on the front page of IT magazines in the developed world. When a bad Chinese copy of the Wii console appears, it is given as a humorous example of the Chinese inability to invent their own products. This way of thinking just goes to strengthen our preconceived notions about people in developing countries as being unable to come up with their own ideas. Petter Andersson, Education Manager at LM Ericsson, which is now facing a competitor that its own customers deem to be more creative, told me, "Many Westerners think that all the Chinese can do is copy and that we in the West are creative. This kind of thinking is dangerous."

We have to learn to copy more – in the sense of looking at what others have done and learning from them. The Chinese travelled around the world searching for the 'best small town in the world' and they found Sigtuna in Sweden. Nowadays, 30,000 Chinese live in a newly built copy of Sigtuna on the outskirts of Shanghai. By studying how other countries have created successful communities, the Chinese built up a knowledge bank. They can then extract ideas from this bank and develop them into their own innovative solutions.

Amelia Hendra was raised in Indonesia, educated in Singapore and now works as a graphic designer in Shanghai. She spends hours and hours on the Internet studying what designers around the globe are doing – in both developing and developed countries. Her aim is to learn and be inspired. Her advice to the designers in developed countries summarizes the attitude that I came across in many creative people in the developing world: **"All you talk about is Copyright, instead you have to learn how to copy right."**

In the West, we are terrified of being accused of ruining someone else's reputation or infringing the copyright of someone else as copyright protects your idea and creativity from being pirated. Of course, what Amelia means is that we need to develop the ability to copy things in the right way; to look at what others are doing and evaluate it, seeing what the good points are. We have to understand how we can best use the ideas of others so that we can then go on to create something better and more innovative ourselves. Which of these two is likely to be the most creative? The person who is good at seeing what others are doing and then combining these ideas into something original – or the person who does not look at what others are doing and thinks that she or he is the most creative and therefore has nothing to learn from anyone else?

People who claim that others do not inspire them are hypocrites, liars or blind, deaf and naïve. Or, as Picasso once said, "Good artists copy. Great artists steal."

A wide variety of exciting innovations are being created in developing countries at the moment and we would benefit from studying them. They are being produced in developing countries because they are not as stuck in set patterns as we are.

Newledge – seeing new solutions by not being trapped in the old ones

I have been living in developing countries for over four years now and one of the most frequent questions I get asked when I come home to Sweden is: "What is going to happen to the environment and the world when the Indians and the Chinese start buying cars?" A very relevant question – but reading between the lines I can detect a feeling that it is wrong for the Chinese and Indians to buy cars. The reasoning goes something like this, "It's OK if we keep our cars, but if they get cars too, then what?"

The creation of a long-term sustainable world in which its assets are more equally distributed is, perhaps, our greatest common challenge right now. My personal opinion is that the solutions to major problems like this one will come from the people in the developing world – and not from us. **Our strategy of trying to stop others from getting what we have will not work.** I am fully aware of the gigantic environmental problems facing China as they race towards riches and welfare. We should not be examining their ability to copy, in record time, the environmentally destructive development we went through in the 20th century. It is much more fascinating to study how quickly they understand the advantages of developing long-term, sustainable solutions. The smoke belching out from the many coal-driven industries in China hides the more interesting parallel development where China is rapidly becoming one of the global leaders of renewable sources of energy.

Erik Wickström is a Swedish venture capitalist, who moved to Beijing three years ago. His company Cleanworld is a part of the explosive Chinese development within the areas of environmental technology and renewable energy solutions. "China is building up its economy just like the West did," he told me. "They are using the cheapest forms of energy like coal, oil and gas. At the same time, however, they are also creating assets in the form of alternative energy. China is the world's largest user of solar-powered water heaters, has the largest growth within wind power, is the world's biggest producer of hydraulic power and is a global leader in the field of solar panels."

People in developing countries find it easier to adopt new solutions. A concrete example of this can be seen on the streets of Beijing. Ten years ago, the sheer number of bikes fascinated many Westerners. Nowadays, they are just as impressed by all the cars and are surprised by how 'developed' Beijing has become. However, those who live in Beijing are more interested in all the electric mopeds they see whooshing past them soundlessly on the streets. Unlike the inhabitants of Western cities, people in Beijing are not hung up on the thought that petrol-driven vehicles are the only alternative. As the Western world mumbles cautiously that it is soon time to exchange petrol-driven cars for electric ones, tens of thousands of Beijingers have already turned words into action and bought themselves an electric vehicle of some sort. They have soundlessly overtaken their Western neighbours when it comes to development. Compared with petrol mopeds, electric ones are cheaper to buy and run, not to mention quieter too. They do not smell or pollute and they go just as fast in an urban environment. Quite simply, electric mopeds are a much better alternative in nearly all areas when you want a cheap way to get to work. A lot of people charge their vehicles' batteries at work so that they do not even have any 'fuel' costs. Just as the Chinese were ready to go from bicycle to electric moped when the technology was far enough advanced to be able to offer a competitive alternative, so too do they find it easier to adopt new solutions. Their ability to see the new is not blinded by their knowledge of old technology. **Time and time again, I have witnessed this ability to absorb new knowledge in many of the developing countries I have visited.**

Let's take South Korea, for example. Jean K. Min, who founded the online citizen journalism newspaper OhmyNews in South Korea, points out the differences between how the South Koreans and the developed world took to the Internet. The Internet arrived in South Korea later than it did in Europe and the USA so that it had gone from being a publishing tool to a collaborative and creative one. According to Jean K. Min, many Americans and Europeans still regard the Internet as being a place where established media publish their material. When the Internet had its breakthrough in these countries, its use developed over several years, which gave media corporations and other traditional content providers the chance to build up their presence on the Net. This is how content for Western users of the Internet was created.

Things happened much more quickly when the South Koreans got access to the Internet: suddenly there were very many South Korean users but very little traditional content. In the meantime, the Internet had developed and Web 2.0 tools and peer-to-peer services could be found. So, instead of seeing the Internet as a passive service, it was more natural for South Korean users to take the new user-generated tools to create their own content. The result is that how South Koreans see the Internet is quite different to the viewpoint of most people in the West. This difference can be seen quite clearly in services like OhmyNews, where thousands of normal people report the news and write articles. It is a news channel by and for users, where private individuals and not journalists generate the news. OhmyNews is a good example of how Korea became a world leader in user-generated content.

The ability to see how something new can be used typifies a developing person, as she or he is not stuck in an out-of-date mindset. I call this 'newledge': knowledge about the new. How good are you at seeing what new things can be used for and to what extent does your old knowledge limit you? The fear of trying out something new can be just as limiting as being set in old ways of thinking as this is the fear of losing what you already have.

Nothing to lose

"We have nothing to lose." That is probably one of the most frequent explanations I hear from people in developing countries when I ask them why they are willing to take such big risks. This goes for most people – whether they work at a small start-up looking to break into an established market or are individuals willing to try out new solutions in order to catch up with developed countries. The opposite is also true: people who have a lot to lose can be reluctant to take risks in order to develop new solutions. So, instead of coming up with new, improved solutions they put their efforts into protecting what they already have.

Lami Yigit, a young Turkish architect, reflected over how only a handful of the people he met when he lived in Europe were willing to sacrifice what they had in order gain something better compared to those living in Turkey. He also pointed out that political guidance in the developed world played a part in this as people who think that what they have is good are more likely to meet politicians' suggestions for change with more scepticism. In other words, they think that change will ruin what they have. **This 'a bird in the hand is worth two in the bush' kind of mentality stops them from trying to capture an even more beautiful bird.**

Ravi Abeyesekera, manager of mobile bank services at the operator Dialog in Sri Lanka described the effect of such fear. As I mentioned earlier, Dialog was one of the first companies in the world to launch mobile payment solutions. In fact, fully developed payment solutions were first launched in developing countries like Sri Lanka, Bangladesh, Zimbabwe, the Philippines and South Africa – and not in developed countries. According to Ravi, operators in developing countries have an advantage because their customers do not know what to expect and, therefore, their expectations of such services are not that high.

If, on the other hand, a company has a large and well-established customer base used to a certain type of service, then launching a new, improved service can be risky if it does not live up to the expectations that customers already have. The end result is that established companies do not dare launch new services, even if they can offer customers a much better service than the one they already have.

This same tendency means that well-known brands are becoming more and more cowardly in their marketing as they are over-enthusiastic about not taking a 'wrong' step. Many advertising firms have had to throw provocative campaigns into the trash can because the customers are afraid of damaging their brands' good reputation. By not wanting to make a mistake, they are creating a 'non-wrong' mistake instead of doing something right.

How can we encourage people to let go of what they have in order to get something that is even better? This is probably the greatest challenge that both company managers and politicians have in the developed world. And how can you best explain to those who are afraid to lose what they have that this is a necessary part of change?

There is an old story about how to catch a monkey by putting a piece of fruit or some nuts in a box with a small hole. When the monkey puts its hand into the hole and grabs the food, its fist is larger than the hole and it cannot get it out again. As the monkey does not want to lose its food, it sits there and can be easily caught. Now, I do not know if the story is true (probably not) but it describes very clearly how dangerous it can be to stick with what you have got instead of letting go. **At the moment, it feels as if many in developing countries are sitting there, desperately holding onto their fruit.**

If you concentrate on keeping things the way they are then you miss out on the chance to improve on them. If you do not go looking for better solutions than the ones you already have, then you run the risk of not seeing that the world has already changed.

Seeing the change

If you live in a country that is prone to earthquakes, then you can see how the ground shakes and how things suddenly change position. If you live in another country and read about that same earthquake in a newspaper, you might be able to guess how much the earth shook. However, you will never have the same understanding and insight, of course, as someone who was actually on the scene at the time. The same thing applies to the changes that are going on in developing countries right now. If you read about them, then you know that they are occurring but that is not the same thing as actually experiencing them for yourself.

We can exemplify this by examining the life of two 28-year-olds. John was born in, say, Oslo in 1980 and Kim was born in Beijing the same year. Now let's think about how much Oslo has changed while John was growing up, and how much Kim's Beijing has changed during the same time. Oslo would have changed, of course, but compared to the enormous changes that Beijing has undergone during this period, you could almost say that Oslo has stood still. So, who can see the global changes more easily? John, who has grown up in a slowly changing Oslo, or Kim, who has spent his youth in a frenziedly-growing Beijing?

Changes are not just about how cities have changed physically: the social changes that developing countries have experienced are just as significant. For example, only a few years ago, homosexuality officially did not exist in China and it was illegal. Nowadays, you can find video blogs about being gay on some of China's largest portals. One mother, who blogged about her experiences as the mother of a son who came out of the closet, became a minor celebrity. It took the West about a century to go from being an agricultural society, where nearly everyone lived and worked in the countryside, to become an urban society. In many developing countries, this change takes place in just a generation. Living in the part of the world that changes most makes it easier to see and understand these changes. In other words, many people in developing countries have experienced major changes.

Mattias Hansson, the trendsetting journalist and CEO of the digital media education company Hyper Island, said this after his visit to Brazil, "Brazilian entrepreneurs are so used to change (as the conditions under which they operate are always changing) that they can alter course in the blink of an eye – go in a new direction, if necessary."

In Seoul, I met the CEO of KPMG in South Korea, Ken Yun. He had an interesting way of describing companies in developed and developing countries. **"As South Korea is a developing country that is not yet complete, there are a lot of holes that need to be filled. We focus on solving these problems – filling in the holes. The result is that we find new solutions every time we discover a new hole. In the developed world, you already think that you have filled all the holes, although that isn't true. Because when the world moves, new holes appear."**

So, living in a world that sees itself as developed means that we miss the changes going on around us, especially if these changes are happening in places where we are not used to looking. At the moment, the world is undergoing drastic changes in many different ways and in places where we least expect it. And this means that there are many holes that need to be filled. Another Korean I spoke to about the Koreans' ability to experience and understand change was Jean K. Min of the online citizen journalism newspaper OhmyNews. "We are used to rapid change, to a breakneck speed of growth. Everything is changing and we do not want to be left out. We Koreans live with high stress levels when it comes to change. We feel a gnawing anxiety as we are so used to noticing change." South Koreans notice how fast the world is altering and this creates constant anxiety – for both good and bad. A rapidly changing world can be stressful and all these new ideas and possibilities can easily create feelings of resignation or frustration. However, it is hard to stop human development, even if the rapid tempo of innovation where millions more people come up with creative ideas is not always beneficial.

But changes occur. This is a fact. And it is impossible to stop the new. No doubt all those who are curious enough to try to keep up will undergo more stress than those who just ignore these changes.

However, living in denial or ignorance of how rapidly things are changing is not a good alternative either. It has never been more important than it is now to study what is going on, and to notice and understand these changes.

Who is best prepared for an earthquake – the person who is worried about the earth moving yet who has the ability to see new holes and understand what they mean? Or the person who has stopped looking for holes in the belief that the world has stopped changing? The world is in constant motion right now and many new gaps are appearing. Can you see them? Do you understand how, where and with what to fill them?

Those who can see the new possibilities that are being created have an advantage over those who cannot. And those who can act on the possibilities they see have an even greater advantage.

Just do it:
The value of **getting things done**

Someone I interviewed in India used Nike's slogan 'Just do it!' to explain the difference between living in a developing country and a developed one. "In the West, you lie in your beds thinking, 'OK. Come on now. Time to get up and go out for a run. Just do it.' You have to force yourselves to go out running. In India, on the other hand, we are already awake. All we have to do is put on the right shoes and run. This is the difference between a developing economy and a developed one. You can see the energy everywhere – so many of us are positive and raring to go."

The technology company Lenovo is a developing company that gets things done. This attitude permeates everything, even their view of innovation. Jean Cai, who works with branding and communications at Lenovo China, explained it like this. "We never do innovation for the sake of innovation, as it is not the target. We are more result oriented and target driven. We want to get things done. We don't talk about innovation – we just do it." Jean then went on to say that even though innovation is a core value at Lenovo and they communicate this both internally and externally, it must never be the one thing that they talk most about. Innovation is something you should do and the focus here is on doing things, not on planning what might get done some time in the future.

"I never plan," said Jack Ma, the founder of Alibaba.com, the world's largest online B2B marketplace. Those three words summarize how important it is to get things done instead of spending too much time on planning what to do. If two people compete in a race and one is planning to get up out of bed and put his shoes on while the other is already running, then the person running will come first. Naturally, this does not mean that planning is wrong. I just mean that the orienteer who is forever looking at the map will not win. The winner is the person who runs fastest in the right direction while looking at the map once in a while to make sure he is running the right way.

While I was in Seoul, I met Lars Vargö, the Swedish ambassador in South Korea. He told me that one of the most important things people in the developed world could learn from the South Koreans was to set goals and then just get started. They are full of initiative and are not afraid of making decisions. When I asked him where developing countries were headed, he thought for a while before answering. **"I feel as if they are on the way to the unknown."**

So, while South Korea and other developing nations are rushing towards the unknown, where is the Western world headed? An acquaintance of mine called Gun Britt told me that one morning she asked her neighbour if she would like to go out jogging that evening. The answer was "no" because the neighbour had already taken a shower earlier that day. Too many people and organizations spend too much time on trivia that do not have any effect on getting things done. How much time do you spend on planning to do something as opposed to actually doing it? How much time do you spend studying the map as opposed to just running fast? How much do you get done – and how much fun do you have while doing so?

The Japanese Idei Nobuyuki was Chairperson for Sony during its glory days when the company was one of the world's most creative organizations and Japan surprised the world with its rapid development, innovation and high-quality products. When Idei and I met at a conference where we were both lecturing, he described the problems that Japan and many large Japanese companies were having. He saw the problem as an illness and divided the symptoms into four letters that made up the abbreviation ABCD. A stands for 'Aged', B for 'Bureaucratic', C for 'Closed' and D for 'Domestic'. According to him, Japan as well as many of its companies have become older and less willing to change, more bureaucratic and closed in their view of the world. Idei Nobuyuki is himself about 70 years old, so when he talks about ageing companies, he means mental ageing, not physical. In fact, his description of Japan is an apt description of the symptoms shown by a developed nation. Idei spoke passionately about what he deems to be necessary medicine for this illness – and, once again, he divided it up into ABC. This time, A stands for 'Active', B for 'Business creation' and C for 'Cross-border interaction'. Idei's point here is that in order to be successful, companies and countries need to have employees and inhabitants that are open to the world around them, that are creative and, above all, that possess the ability to actively implement those changes that they are inspired to bring about. He was very worried indeed about those who did not have these qualities.

It is the animals that can adapt themselves to the changes in nature that survive. In much the same way, people who make the necessary changes are the ones who are most successful. Often, those who see themselves as upstarts or challengers are the ones who find it easiest to make these changes.

Refusing to be the largest

A developing company refuses to say that it is the largest. Or the best. A developing person refuses to say she is successful. 'Kenny the fish' and his company Qian Hu Corporation is a wonderful example of this. Kenny the fish is the Executive Chairman and founder of Qian Hu Corporation, the world's largest breeder of ornamental fish. His real name is Kenny Yap Lee, but everyone – including himself – uses the name Kenny the fish. He does not talk about his line of business in terms of 'animal breeding' or 'fish farming'. No – he says things like, "We are a service provider of life style products" or "We are a knowledge-based industry." He went on to explain that a lot of innovation and knowledge is needed to raise and transport ornamental fish around the world without these small, fragile creatures dying along the way. And they do die – easily. Qian Hu's logo is a grim reminder of this fact: the logo is a fish called the high fin loach. When Kenny founded his company in 1989, it was a fish farm and one of the first things he did was to buy in 4,000 High Fin Loaches for the sum of 400,000 Singapore dollars. All four thousand fish died in the space of a few dramatic weeks and the company nearly went under before it had even started. So, the company decided to have the High Fin Loach as its logo. As Kenny put it, "Our logo is worth 400,000 dollars. It is a very expensive reminder that success is never easy." The company survived and today it is a world leader when it comes to breeding and exporting ornamental fish. It has subsidiaries in several different Asian countries. **However, Kenny refuses to say that they are the 'biggest'. As a developing company, he sees their role like this: "We are not a big fish in a small lake. We are a slightly larger fish in the big sea."**

According to him, it is important not to look at the line of business you are in, but instead, to focus on making your own company the best it can be. For as he says, "There are no 'sunrise' businesses." Meaning that when the sun rises in one place, it sets somewhere else. And once the sun has risen, it then moves position across the sky. In other words, everything changes, and that is why he refuses to define himself as the largest. He even objected when I said that he was successful in spite of the fact that he has won a whole range of awards including 'Entrepreneur of the Year' in Singapore.

"You can't call yourself successful until you have retired and recruited a management board that is better than yourself. It's like being a parent: you don't know until you die whether you have raised your kids well so that they don't fight over their inheritance."

Ron Sim has also been awarded 'Entrepreneur of the Year' in Singapore. He is the founder and CEO of Osim, a company that develops innovative, healthy lifestyle products, including their own specially-designed massage products. Osim is another good example of a developing company that refuses to say it has met all of its goals. A few years ago, their goal was to open 1,000 stores, but before they achieved this, they changed the goal to 3,000 stores instead. What is important here is that Ron changed the goal before it was reached because a developing company never allows itself to 'reach its objective'. Just like Ron Sim, these kinds of companies know that if they reach their goals, then they run the risk of relaxing and losing momentum to enjoy the feeling of having won. So, a developing company is an organization that is always moving towards a goal. And even though Osim says it is a global leader when it markets itself, Ron points out that they always communicate the opposite within the company. "You can say things like that as part of a marketing strategy – but never internally. If someone were to tell me that we are number one, my reply would be, 'So – we're number one? So what! There's still so much to do!'" You might be wondering if it is not a little dangerous never to allow people to experience the feeling of achievement; to never let them rest. Ron said that this was a common objection from people in developed countries; one that is based on a misunderstanding. The whole point is not to push the employees into running faster and faster, but to build up an organization that is in constant motion; one with a tempo that means you do not have to stop and rest. Sitting there in Ron's modern, air-conditioned office on a warm Singaporean day, I suddenly saw a similarity between what he was saying and a Marathon. The winner does not stop and rest, but keeps a steady tempo so that he still has energy to complete the race. The amateurs runs too quickly in the beginning and then have to take breathers at every rest stop, which makes it more and more difficult to get started again. These are the people who are then disqualified when the track is closed after a certain period of time.

At first, it felt cynical when the CEO of the world's largest organization in a line of business that is all about relaxing talked about the importance of never resting. But when I understood how he encouraged his employees to keep a steady pace that was sustainable in the long term without having to stop and pat themselves on the back for their good work, it felt like a refreshing attitude and one that is worth imitating.

Even Du Jianhua, Vice-President and General Manager, China Infrastructure, at Lenovo shares the same way of thinking. Lenovo happily talks about challenging the two global giants Dell and Hewlett Packard. Du Jianhua told me, "Our determination to be first is enormous." At the same time, he has understood the value of never stopping. Du Jianhua described very poetically how he wants Lenovo to be perceived as a global brand, "We want to be a tree in the forest of the most-admired companies." When I objected by saying that they were already an admired company, with a strong brand on many of the most important computer markets – not to mention the fact that Lenovo is already the world's third largest computer manufacturer, Du Jianhua reacted strongly. When they became the largest PC brand in China, a lot of focus was placed on winning ground on markets in the rest of the world. Lenovo gets its energy from being seen as the underdog and it does not want to be perceived as one of the largest. He summarized the attitude that is common among many managers of developing companies with these words, **"If you're number one, it's too easy to become arrogant. A lot of big companies have been beaten by smaller ones because they got too big-headed."**

A lot of the energy you can feel in developing countries comes from the collective feeling of being a challenger or upstart. This attitude can be seen in many of the inhabitants of these countries too. And perhaps we, in the developed world, can learn most from this strong, positive human energy that you can find in developing countries.

The energy

When I ask people who have moved to developing countries what fascinated them most when they arrived, they often say, "The energy." When I ask people from developed countries who have moved back home after a spell in a developing country what they miss the most, they reply, "The energy." And when I ask people living in developing countries what they think gives them a competitive edge, they declare, "Our energy."

After visiting more than twenty developing countries in three continents, I can only confirm that the greatest impression they left on me is the energy they all have. Naturally, the developed world has its share of liveliness, but these scattered bouts of energy in the West cannot be compared to the vast energy that you can find everywhere in the developing world. It is so strong that you can almost reach out and touch it.

Chris Lee, a designer from Singapore who has travelled a lot in developing countries, described it well when he said, "I don't think the West is slowing down. It's just that the East is speeding up so much faster. Everyone wants to do something new here. Everyone wants to create the next big trend. This creates a lot of energy and this energy is infectious. And when a lot of different people with different ideas and energy get together, they start to vibrate and you get this feeling that anything is possible."

I wondered where all this energy would lead. According to Chris, the fact that developing countries do not have a long history of rapid development means that development does not often proceed along a straight or clear line. **"When you have nothing to look back on, you run in different directions. But that also creates excitement and energy. It is boring when everyone does the same thing. Here we feel as if we can do whatever we like."**

There are many ways of looking at the factors that lead to creativity. One is that you have to give people tools, technologies and processes in order to be creative. Another is to claim that genuine creativity arises out of hunger, the desire to change, a determination to create something; that creativity comes from energy.

It is possible that the developed world has more tools, technologies and processes for being innovative. But it is easy to see who is the hungriest, and has the strongest desire to change and the fiercest determination to create something new. You can find this sort of energy in developing countries. You cannot create anything with energy alone. But it is equally true to say that nothing significant has been created without it.

Too many people in developed countries live in a world without energy. Which world do you live in? A world teeming with excitement or a world without it? How does this affect you? Because if energy is infectious, what about the lack of it?

I am not yet sure if it is energy that makes people curious or if it is curiosity that creates energy. But I know that energy and curiosity are two qualities that the people in developing nations possess, and it is clear that those of us who live in the developed world should learn from them.

Curiosity

Gordon Gao is the Account Director of the Executive Education Department and CIBS (China Europe International Business School). According to the Financial Times, CIBS is the eleventh best MBA school in the world and the best one in Asia. And, as it is the top Asian business school with a campus in Shanghai, it is only natural that it attracts some of China's leading business entrepreneurs as well as increasing numbers of foreign students who want to get a better understanding of what is happening in the world's largest country. In his capacity as the director of the Executive Education Department, Gordon Gao knows a lot of these students, and he can see major differences between those that come from developing countries and those that do not. **"For many in the West, their curiosity is not as strong as it was in their forefathers.** A developed person is just like a developed country: it tends to stop learning new things. When people like this come across a new idea, a new culture or a new product, their response tends to be, 'I know everything worth knowing and as I don't know anything about this, then why should I bother with it?' You see, we humans have a habit of enjoying our success, but this enjoyment tends to make us stop and then we forget to move on."

Gordon claims that the students from developing nations that attend CIBS are far more curious than their Western counterparts. He emphatically believes that the ability to move forward, to always want to develop and the desire to learn are just as much human qualities as our desire to rest on our laurels. However, the desire to develop demands more of us, and there is the risk of being frightened by the unknown. "It is not easy to move on because a lot of uncertainties lie ahead. We do not know what awaits us in the future, while the things we have now feel safe. It feels dangerous to move towards the unknown as we are afraid of meeting things that we cannot control."

Gordon is passionate about helping people to develop constantly, to understand the value of always being curious and to keep on learning. He practises what he preaches. He reads five books a month and can often be seen in the school's library picking up a new book. He tries to choose at least one book per month on a subject that he does not think he is interested in, just to broaden his learning. And every Friday afternoon, he meets his colleagues to study a range of differing subjects. One afternoon might be spent exploring Shakespeare's English; the next is devoted to memorizing classical Chinese poems or listening to a guest professor talking about the latest management theories. The aim of these afternoon meetings is to create a cross-learning experience. He said: "I think we should push ourselves to learn something new on a daily basis. Every day we must ask ourselves: 'Have I learnt something new today? Have I read a new book or heard about a great idea that I had never thought of?'"

I asked Gordon, as a developing person, to give some advice to those in developed countries who feel that they are stagnating. The reply he gave was unexpected. Instead of addressing his answer to the Western world, he directed his advice to the Chinese and to those in developing countries: "We Chinese are interested in knowing more about developed countries like those in Europe or the USA. But have we paid enough attention to Russia? Are we learning all we can from Brazil, Vietnam, Nigeria and Egypt? Can we learn something from them? Of course we can! Have we done so? No, we haven't!"

He warned people in developing countries with these words, "Watch out! We will call ourselves developed countries one day, if we're not careful. We must never stop learning from others; **we must never stop being curious.**"

We are all born curious. As soon as a baby has learnt to focus, she cannot stop exploring her surroundings. A small child wants to experience everything through his mouth and puts in everything that looks good much to the agony of his worried parents. A slightly older child looks at a fruit with curiosity and wants to know, "Can I eat that?" while an adult examines the fruit dubiously and wonders if it is OK to eat. When we were six, we were entranced by something as simple as an ant carrying its burden of a pine needle; but somewhere along the way, most of us lost this enquiring fascination when we became adults. According to Gordon Gao and many others with experience of people from both the developing and the developed world, this kind of curiosity is strongest right now in developing countries.

Professor Amarnath has also noticed this lack of curiosity. We talked about this very subject on a car journey between Mumbai and Pune on the way to an innovation conference together. He looked at me with sorrowful eyes and said, **"The sense of wonder in the developed world is gone."** It is not he who should be sad – but us.

If you define yourself as developed and therefore think that you have come further than your competitors while also believing that you cannot invent anything else, then you are just doubling your resistance to curiosity. If you think the opposite instead: that you are still developing and more open to the new – and more curious – then you can create new trends that develop and grow more quickly. This is what is happening in developing countries right now.

Just as a young person can remind an old one how fascinating the world can be, so too must we in the developed world let the developing nations remind us of the value of retaining our curiosity; of always being fascinated by what is going on around us – in our world and in other parts too. Actively nurture and grow your curiosity: not only because curiosity is probably one of the most valuable abilities you could possess in the rapidly changing world of today, but also because it is this curiosity that drives our human development. And it is this that has, to a large extent, brought us to where we find ourselves today. **A young Turkish designer said it so well when I talked to her in Istanbul, "If you don't look for new things – then what are you living for?"**

In a world that is changing more and more rapidly, the quality of being curious about the latest developments becomes more valuable. It takes a special kind of curiosity, though. It is a curiosity about what is going on right now. I call it 'nowriosity'. It is not enough to be curious in a general sense because to be a developing person you must also be especially interested in the new ideas that are being created. How do get information about what is going on in the world? Where do you find your inspiration? How curious are you about the developments happening in the world – the whole world – at the moment?

Is 'good enough' **better?**

Sometimes on my visits home to Sweden in recent times, I get the feeling that many people in developed countries (like Sweden) believe that the swift development that has occurred in recent years in the developing world has now peaked. As if there is some sort of law that says that developing countries can catch up with us but not overtake us. But what if they did not only catch up, but also overtook us? Someone who catches up with the leader of a marathon very seldom contents herself with just catching up. In fact, the challenger usually has a quick burst of energy and pulls ahead. The feeling I get when talking to people in developing countries is that they will not at all be satisfied with just keeping up with what we have managed to achieve. And they are not happy with the speed at which they are catching up either. They are running very fast at the moment, but want to go even faster.

Joachim Rosenberg, manager of Volvo Trucks Asia, put into words why speed matters. "At Volvo, we estimate that our competitors are moving about four or five times faster than we are. So, in five years they will have developed 15 to 20 years. When friends visit us from Sweden, they usually say, 'Wow! A lot has happened since I was last here.' I usually reply, 'You haven't been away for a year – you've been gone for five.'"

A Chinese woman I interviewed in Beijing works at a large company that is half Swedish and which has been around since the beginning of the 1900s. "My bosses tell me to slow down," she told me. "They think that I work too quickly." The company is doing well, but the woman is not impressed. In fact, she is worried by the sluggishness she notices in her organization, but she finds it hard to put her feelings into words. After a long pause, she finally finds a simile she is happy with. **"Many Asian companies behave like young men. This company, like many other European ones, behaves like an old man."**

Others have drawn similar parallels, but I still object and say that the old man does not necessarily have to lose to the younger one. She replied: "Well, I think the future of the young man is brighter than the future of the old one – wouldn't you agree?"

She has a point. Companies that learn to act more like young, curious people live longer. In a world that is changing furiously day by day, then the importance of knowing what was done before loses its value. Learning new things and adapting ourselves to meet the new is more valuable than experience these days. The ability of the developing world to run fast and to absorb new things is, perhaps, best seen in South Korea.

Been Kim is 25 years old and works as a product designer at the Korean company LG. "We Koreans are really good at doing things quickly. We might not have the perfect strategy, but we still win because we are much faster." This 'good enough' strategy involves rapidly making a product and then constantly improving it in order to remain one step ahead of the competitors at all times. It means launching a product that is good enough to be launched and sacrificing the time it would have taken to produce a perfect product in order to get it out on the market more quickly. Once the product has been launched, you can then put your energy into producing better versions as you develop them. Many of my interviewees agreed that the speed shown by people and companies in developing nations will turn out to be a greater advantage than most of us in the developed world realize.

In the classic fable about the hare and the tortoise, they race against each other. The hare sits down to rest under a tree because he is so far ahead and believes that he does not have to make an effort to win. However, he falls asleep and the tortoise wins the race. The only difference in reality is that the competitor is not a slow tortoise, but another hare, who can run faster than we realize, and who starts off so far behind that the sleeping hare did not realize what he was up against.

Developed and **developing people**

The purpose of this book is to turn the concept of 'developed' and 'developing' countries upside down, and to help those in developed countries to realize that no country is ever fully developed. In a literal sense, however, a country cannot 'develop' because it is just a legal construction of a geographical area. Rather – it is the people living in a country who must develop themselves, their workplaces and their surroundings so that change can happen.

The same thing applies to organizations. We might think of companies like Apple as being creative and innovative, but that does not mean that everyone working there is an innovative thinker. In the same way, certain state-owned organizations are regarded as being unbending and bureaucratic, but that does not mean that everyone working there is like that. In fact, the majority are probably not. For a company to develop, the people who work there must be willing to change and also be given the chance to bring about change. And for this kind of human development to take place, then people must be the first to change. And for this to happen, people must be open to change.

To illustrate what I mean, I have divided people into two groups: developed people and developing people.

Developed people define things as finished. It can be a professor who does not think she has to keep up with the latest developments in her field as she is already regarded as the leading authority. Or a marketing manager who does not believe he has to learn about the most recent trends in search engine optimization because he only uses traditional advertising channels. It can be a world champion boxer who thinks he does not need to train quite so hard for the next match as, after all, he is the reigning champion and undefeated in the last ten matches. It can also be a parent who does not want to learn how to cook even more dishes as she is already pretty good at varying the weekly menu.

Here is a closer look at what a developed person can be like. I held a one-day workshop for all the managers of a large car sales company.

Before I started my lecture, the CEO introduced me. "It is of vital importance in our business that is undergoing a lot of bankruptcies these days that all managers keep on developing their creative skills so that we can adapt to the ever-changing markets in our line of business. We must never stop developing our innovative thinking, which is why we have asked Fredrik Härén to come here today to inspire us to think in new ways." He looked at me and added, "Unfortunately, I can't be with you today as I have a few things to take care of." Then he left the premises. The message he sent to the group was that everyone had to develop their creativity. Everyone, except for him that is, as he was already completely developed.

The comedian and journalist Erik Blix once told me about a colleague of his at Swedish Radio. This story is a brilliant, yet tragic and extreme, example of a developed person. Erik and his colleague went to a restaurant that was serving venison as its dish of the day. Erik was over the moon, but his companion explained that he did not eat venison. When Erik asked if he was vegetarian or allergic, his colleague replied, "No. I just don't eat things I have never had before. And I have never ever tried venison." At first, Erik thought his friend was joking, but he was dead serious. When he was a teenager, he had already decided that he had tried enough different kinds of food and knew what he liked. Erik and his colleague left the restaurant and went to a pizzeria instead. Jokingly, Erik asked him, "So, you can only eat Capricciosa, right? I bet you can't have a Four Seasons pizza." The man answered without irony, "That's right. I only eat Capricciosa."

We all know people who think of themselves as developed, who have finished learning. I interpret the fact that you have taken the time to read this book as a sign that you are a curious person, who wants to gain a better understanding of what is going on in the world and how these developments affect us. After all, you can live in a developed country full of developed people and still never stop being a developing person. One of the qualities that characterizes successful people is the ability never to see themselves as done, and to push themselves to take on new challenges.

Tiger Woods - as a golfer—is a good example of a developing person. Although almost everyone in the golfing world thinks of him as the world's best golf player, he does not talk about himself in these terms. According to him, Jack Nicklaus is the world's top player with 18 major championships under his belt. Tiger Woods 'only' has 14. This attitude means that Woods does not risk stagnating. His goal is to continue developing as a golf player.

Many of the people I have described in this book are developing people: people who are not satisfied, who are curious, hungry and who dare take risks. They dream big dreams and make sure that as many of these dreams as possible come true. They brim over with energy. They are happy and love life. In other words, they are alive.

The creativity consultant and author, Dilip Mukerjea from Singapore, defines a developing person like this: **"A developing person feels fear and hesitation, but marches forward anyway. She feels a sense of wonder, and has the courage to fail. This person is never satisfied. She isn't starving but she is always hungry for more."**

Dilip himself could have been the role model for this description. He reads ten books a week, has written many books himself, and travels around Asia giving lectures about creativity. When you meet him, he asks endless questions. His experience is that the developing people he often meets have more knowledge than the developed ones – and they still keep on acquiring more. They never stop learning and they never lose their sense of curiosity. And they never stop dreaming.

Of all the inspiring, creative and developing people that I have met over the years, Sachio Senmoto is the best example of what it means to be a developing person. Sachio is not young; he is more than 60. He does not come from a developing country; he comes from Japan. He has not spent his entire life as a wild entrepreneur constantly developing new ideas. Quite the opposite: he worked for the large Japanese telecoms operator NTT DOCOMO until he was 40. Then he blossomed. He gave up his nice, safe job at NTT DOCOMO, became an entrepreneur and started competing against his former employer. He founded several companies, which he then went on to sell for millions of dollars. And although his friends thought he was crazy when he resigned from his job, Sachio's whole point is that you cannot live happily if you live without taking risks. He is a perfect example of this: an effervescent, happy old man full of energy and ideas, and who is still starting up new companies even though he has passed retirement age.

In spite of his success, he stressed that he was not special. In fact, he claims to be just an ordinary person, with the same potential as everyone else. He is passionate about helping people fulfil their potential and always continuing to develop themselves. He took my hand to indicate just how important it was that I really understood what he realized so late in life: **"If you don't make your dreams come true, then you are only living 1% of your full potential."**

Conclusion

Michelangelo once said: **"The greater danger for most of us lies not in setting our aim too high and falling short; but in setting our aim too low, and achieving our mark."** I wonder what he would have thought of the expression 'developed' country.

Earlier on in the book, I mentioned that 70% of the people living in a developed country like Sweden do not believe that life will improve in the future. And yet, in many surveys about the best countries in the world to live in, Sweden is usually at the top – often in fifth or sixth place, and Norway is very often number one on these lists. When I visited Norway recently to give a lecture to more than 150 top managers in Norwegian export industries, not a single person put up a hand when I asked if they thought Norway would be a better country tomorrow than it is today. It is, of course, quite a feat for two insignificant countries in cold, northern Europe to succeed in creating some of the world's best countries to live in. However, that does not mean that there is no room for improvement. We have bought into our own myths that we are so well developed that we just cannot advance any further.

Never before has the world developed at such a rapid pace as it is doing now, and this development is only going to increase as more and more creative, enterprising and ambitious people in developing countries get the possibility to contribute their creative skills. In this context, the label developed strikes me as being the silliest and most limiting thing we can use to define ourselves. Instead, we have to create a feeling of collaboration, of wanting to participate; and we have to continue developing the developed world too.

The world faces challenges of enormous proportions when billions of people in developing countries – at a furious pace – want to participate in and share the wellbeing that is being created. The solutions we have come up with so far are just not good enough. We already use more of the earth's resources than the earth can produce. The solution cannot – and must not – be to try to stop certain people from sharing the wealth. And anyway, they would not accept this solution.

We have to create new solutions, find new ways of coping with both old and new problems and urge ourselves to change the way we view what we do, how we do it and how we could do it in the future. To put it simply, we have to be more creative.

In a changed world like ours we cannot afford it if that part of the world that many have looked up to for leadership and direction now finds itself in a kind of collective inability to take action and where we defend what we have. We cannot afford to look at what is going on in developing countries either and dismiss them as merely problems. Developing countries lag behind in many areas and are facing gigantic problems. They do things wrong; they can be unprofessional and undemocratic. It is up to us to help them solve these problems. At the same time, we must let them help us with our problems. We may live in one of the best countries, but I do not think that any Swede (or European) would go as far as saying that our society is ideal and that we could not be healthier, happier, more satisfied and whole as people. Nor would we claim that the world could not be made even better.

Looking back on what people have done earlier will not solve our problems in the future. We cannot possibly see our way to new solutions by just saying that others have done things in a worse way than we have. And the world will never be a better place if we believe that we already have all the answers.

On one occasion, while doing research for this book, I found myself in Iceland. While I was there, I heard about the Icelandic word heimskur. It is a concept that means idiot. The word supposedly comes from the Viking age. **A heimskur was a Viking who had never left his home to embark on journeys to foreign countries and who, therefore, missed out on new ways of thinking about how things could be done. In the eyes of the Icelandic Vikings, you became an idiot by just sitting around at home, believing that you already knew how things could be done in the best way.** By staying at home, you end up not daring to try new things and, by doing so, make your world a very narrow one. This can lead to even more unfortunate results: for a limited person is someone who does not dream very much and who does not try to make any dreams come true.

During the interviews I conducted with more than 200 people in 20 different countries, I nearly always concluded the interviews by asking what we in the developed world could learn from the people in developing countries. The most frequent answer was, **"You have to be more curious."**

So, I choose to end this book with the same words. We have to be more curious. Curious about what is going on in the world. Eager to know what these changes mean. Curious enough to look at how people in other countries choose to define and solve problems. Enthusiastic enough to manage to question how we choose to do things at home. And daring enough to dare to dream about how the world could be an even better place to live. And then we need to be brave enough and strong enough to implement those ideas. Because the world is far from being developed.

So never become a developed person.

The Developing World **Manifesto**

You are the developed world.
I am the developing world.

You think that most things have been developed.
I look for new opportunities.

You look to your own part of the world for good ideas.
I look everywhere for the best ideas.

You know all about your world.
I know all about my world. And yours.

You are stuck in the old infrastructure.
I absorb and adopt the latest technology.

You teach.
I learn.

You try to protect what you have got.
I am determined to get what is mine.

Your dream for tomorrow is to keep the status quo.
I am dreaming great dreams – and making them come true.

Change makes you uncomfortable.
For me, it is as natural as breathing.

You are used to being in the lead.
You take it for granted.
You think that this gives you an advantage,
And you say it will take us a hundred years to catch up.

I know better.

You live in the developed world.
I live in the developing world.

You do not know where you are headed.
I am already embracing my dreams.

Join me.

Leave The Developed World.
Become part of The Developing World.

The author

Fredrik Härén is the founder of The Interesting Organization (interesting.org) – one of Sweden's leading creativity companies. He is the author of seven books. His Idea Books have been translated into more than 15 languages, and was recently included in the american book "The 100 Best Business Books of All Time".

Fredrik is a renowned speaker and has given over 1,000 lectures in 30 countries. He was voted Speaker of the Year 2007 in Sweden together with his twin brother Teo Härén.

Fredrik lived in Beijing from December 2005 until April 2008 when he moved to Singapore where he now lives. He often holds lectures and workshops in Europe as well as in Asia.

While carrying out research for this book, he travelled to 20 countries, including developing countries like Lithuania, Estonia, Russia, South Africa, Thailand, Singapore, Malaysia, Indonesia, the Maldives, India, Sri Lanka, China, South Korea, Turkey and Laos. He has also travelled to developed countries like Iceland, Sweden, Japan, Norway, Great Britain, the USA and France. What thoughts and ideas did you have while reading this book? Have you discussed the book's theme with others?

Please share your viewpoints with him at:
fredrik.haren@interesting.org

Do you want more information about what is happening in the world? Send an e-mail to: tdw@interesting.org to get more stories and information. Do not forget to check out Fredrik's lecture on YouTube: http://www.youtube.com/user/interestingorg.

Or go to **www.TheDevelopingWorld.com.**

fredrik.haren@interesting.org

Translator

Fiona Miller, an award-winning scriptwriter and author, is the translator of this book. Educated at Cambridge University, she has worked as a teacher around the world and written more than ten educational books for companies such as the BBC, Oxford University Press, Liber AB and Natur & Kultur. She is one of Sweden's most experienced scriptwriters for interactive media.

About
the interesting organisation (interesting.org)

The Interesting Organization is Sweden's leading creativity company and is most active in Northern Europe and Asia. Our vision is to inspire others and each other to get more ideas and make them a reality.

The Interesting Organization helps people and organizations in more than 30 countries to become more innovative and creative. And as no two people or companies are alike, we do this in many different ways. From creative coaching of managerial groups to individual coaching of company presidents; from workshops about how to develop creativity and generate ideas to helping companies develop long-term creativity strategies.

We are also well known for our successful keynote speeches, lectures and workshops about creativity, innovation and idea generation as well as for our best-selling series of Idea Books and other creativity tools.

Contact us at www.interesting.org and let us know what challenges you are facing. We will let you know how we can help you and, of course, provide relevant references from among our thousands of satisfied customers.

About **The Idea Book**

Fredrik Häréns most well known book is "The Idea Book". It is a book and note book designed to help the reader develop his or her creativity. It has sold more than 200,000 copies around the world and has been published in 14 languages, including: English, Japanese and Chinese. The book was so popular in Iceland that 3,000 copies were sold in a month – meaning that it only took 30 days for 1% of the population to come in contact with the book.

The Idea Book was recently included in the American book "The 100 Best Business Books of all Time" by Jack Covert and Todd Sattersten.

Book a lecture or workshop

Invite your co-workers or customers to an inspiring seminar on business creativity. To a lecture about the importance and value of new ideas. Or to an uplifting talk that encourages creativity and innovative thinking.

Fredrik's lectures help the audience understand how valuable it is to think in new ways – and how difficult this is to achieve.

Fredrik was voted Speaker of the Year 2007 in Sweden, so if someone can give a good speech, he can. He lectures around the world and has given speeches to more than 1000 companies and organizations in more than 30 countries ranging from China and Japan to the USA and Canada.

Satisfied customers include The Swedish Parliament, The Swedish Police Force, Hewlett Packard, China Mobile, Ogilvy and American Express and many, many more.

In 2008 Fredrik was selected as one of Sweden´s "10 most sought after b-2-b-speakers.

www.**thedevelopingworld**.com

The book's own web site.